Literacy in Context

Language to
imagine, explore and entertain

Celeste Flower

General editors **Joan Ward** *and* **John O'Connor**
Literacy consultant **Lyn Ranson**
General consultant **Frances Findlay**

PUBLISHED BY THE PRESS SYNDICATE OF THE UNIVERSITY OF CAMBRIDGE
The Pitt Building, Trumpington Street, Cambridge, United Kingdom

CAMBRIDGE UNIVERSITY PRESS
The Edinburgh Building, Cambridge CB2 2RU, UK
40 West 20th Street, New York, NY 10011-4211, USA
10 Stamford Road, Oakleigh, VIC 3166, Australia
Ruiz de Alarcón 13, 28014 Madrid, Spain
Dock House, The Waterfront, Cape Town 8001, South Africa

http://www.cambridge.org

First published 2001

Printed in Italy by Graphicom

Typeface Delima MT 10.5pt on 12.5pt leading   *System* QuarkXPress®

A catalogue record for this book is available from the British Library

ISBN 0 521 80560 0 paperback

Prepared for publication by Pentacor PLC

Cover illustration by Richard Desmarais.
Illustrations by Clive Goodyer (pp.26, 38, 39), Mike Ogden (p.60) and Adam Stower (pp.62, 63, 64).

ACKNOWLEDGEMENTS
The publishers gratefully acknowledge the following for permission to reproduce copyright material.

Textual material Extracts from *Ruby in the Smoke* (p.8) by Philip Pullman (first published by Puffin 1984), by permission of
Scholastic Ltd; *The Away Team* (p.8) by Michael Hardcastle (Egmont Children's Books), by permission of Michael Hardcastle;
Goodnight Mr Tom (pp.14, 15) by Michelle Magorian (first published by Penguin Books, 1980) copyright © Michelle Magorian 1980,
by permission of the author c/o Rogers, Coleridge & White Ltd, 20 Powis Mews, London W11 1JN; *Horrible Histories: The Vile
Victorians* (p.31) by Terry Deary (Scholastic Children's Books), by permission of Scholastic Ltd; *The Philosophy Files* (pp.38, 39) by
Stephen Law (Orion Children's Books), by permission of The Orion Publishing Group Ltd; 'When We Went to the Park' (p.44) from
THE NURSERY COLLECTION © 1985 1986 Shirley Hughes, by permission of Walker Books Ltd, London; THIS IS THE BEAR (p.45)
Text © 1986 Sarah Hayes, Illustrations © 1986 Helen Craig, by permission of Walker Books Ltd, London; QUACKY QUACK QUACK
(p.45) Text © 1991 Ian Whybrow, Illustrations ©1991 Russell Ayto, by permission of Walker Books Ltd, London; *Blackadder: The
Whole Damn Dynasty* (pp.50, 51) by Richard Curtis and Ben Elton (Penguin Books) copyright © Richard Curtis and Ben Elton 1987,
by permission of Michael Joseph 1998; *Letter To Daniel; Despatches From The Heart* (pp.56, 57) by Fergal Keane, copyright © Fergal
Keane 1996, by permission of BBC Worldwide Ltd; 'What has happened to Lulu?' (p.64) from *Collected Poems* by Charles Causley
1970 (Macmillan), by permission of David Higham Associates; *Skellig* (pp.70, 71) by David Almond (Hodder Children's Books), by
permission of Hodder and Stoughton Ltd; *The Village by the Sea* (p.72) by Anita Desai (Heinemann) copyright © Anita Desai 1982,
by permission of the author c/o Rogers, Coleridge & White Ltd, 20 Powis Mews, London W11 1JN; *Buddy* (p.76) by Nigel Hinton
(first published by J M Dent & Sons Ltd 1983, New Windmill Series, Heinemann 1983) copyright ©Nigel Hinton 1982, by
permission of Curtis Brown Ltd, London, on behalf of Nigel Hinton.

Mind Map® (pp.26, 27) is the registered trademark of the Buzan Organisation and is used with enthusiastic permission. To find
out more about Mind Maps contact the Buzan Centre, 54 Parkstone Road, Poole, Dorset BH15 2PG, Tel: 01202 674676,
www.mind_map.com

For the ideas and information for 'Percy the Penguin' (pp.32, 33) the author would like to thank the lower school science
department, Lord Williams's School, Thame.

'The Princess who stood on her own two feet' copyright © Jeanne Desy first appeared in *Stories for Free Children*, ed. L. Pograbin (1982).

Photographs Goodnight Mr Tom (p.15) ref. Goodni~1. TIF(bfi films), by permission of BBC Picture Archives; Assorted images of
people (p.18), by permission of GettyOne Stone; Kenneth Brannagh as Henry V (p.20), Photostage © Donald Cooper, by permission
of Ronald Grant Archives; Emperor Penguins (p.32) ref. AU70/GR, by permission of Ardea, London Ltd; Blackadder (p.50), by
permission of BBC Picture Archives; Edwardian woman: Miss J Martin 1902 (p.56) ref. H114701, by permission of Hulton Getty;
Buddy Holly (p.77), by permission of Ronald Grant Archives.

Every effort has been made to trace copyright holders, but in some cases this has proved impossible. The publishers would be
happy to hear from any copyright holder that has not been acknowledged.

Introduction

- Read a piece of text
- Read it again to discover what makes it special
- Check that you understand it
- Focus on key features
- Learn about the language features and practise using them
- Improve your spelling
- Plan and write your own similar piece
- Check it and redraft

Each unit in this book helps you to understand more about a particular kind of writing, learn about its language features and then work towards your own piece of writing in a similar style.

Grammar, spelling and punctuation activities, based on the extract, will improve your language skills and take your writing to a higher level.

The book at a glance

The texts

The extracts are taken from the National Curriculum reading lists. Each part of the book contains units of extracts and activities at different levels to help you measure your progress.

Each unit includes these sections:

Purpose

This explains exactly what you will read, learn about and write.

Key features

These are the main points to note about the way the extract is written.

Language skills

These activities will improve your grammar and punctuation. They are all based on the extracts. They are organised using the Word, Sentence and Text Level Objectives of the *National Literacy Strategy Framework*.

Planning your own writing

This structured, step-by-step guide will help you to get started, use writing frames and then redraft and improve your work.

Teacher's Portfolio

This includes worksheets for more language practice, revision and homework. Self-assessment charts will help you to judge and record what level you have reached and to set your own targets for improvement.

Contents

Contents

Entertain

Comparing texts

Word	Spelling	Sentence	Text	Activities
• Onomatopoeia	• Adding -ing	• Simple and compound structures • wh- words	• Plot • Rhyme • Rhythm • Repetition	Writing a story for a child under six (word limit of 150 words)
• New words and nonce words	• -tion	• Setting out TV and playscript: punctuation and emphases	• Humour – how misunderstand-ings can add structure to a scene	Creating a short dramatic sketch based on a moment from history
• Euphemism	• -ally	• First person • Commas for parenthesis	• Verb tenses • Chronology • Time adverbials	Writing a section from your own autobiography, in which you remember another person

Word	Spelling	Sentence	Text	Activities
• Rhyme • Half-rhyme • Eye-rhyme • Internal rhyme • Assonance	• -igh	• Direct speech • Reported speech	• Ballad form • Rhyme schemes • Repetition • Refrain	Compose your own ballad
• Linked words • Connotation	• -au-	• Hyphen • Dash	• Closure • Narrative problems • Resolutions • Coda • Sequel	Write an ending for the story that is outlined (coda) Redraft this as an alternative ending (sequel leader)

Opening moves

1 ▸ **Purpose**

In this unit you will:
- read the openings from some novels written for young people
- compare the language and content of different novel types
- write your own novel openings

▸▸ **Subject links:** *history, geography, science, PE, PSHE, media studies*

2 ▸ **Opening paragraphs**

Three novels from different genres

a Ruby in the Smoke

On a cold, fretful afternoon in early October, 1872, a hansom cab drew up outside the offices of Lockhart and Selby, Shipping Agents in the financial heart of London, and a young girl got out and paid the driver.

She was a person of sixteen or so – alone, and uncommonly pretty. She was slender and pale, and dressed in mourning, with a black bonnet under which she tucked back a straying twist of blonde hair that the wind had teased loose. She had unusually dark brown eyes for one so fair. Her name was Sally Lockhart; and within fifteen minutes, she was going to kill a man.

Philip Pullman

b The princess who stood on her own two feet

A long time ago in a kingdom by the sea there lived a Princess tall and bright as a sunflower. Whatever the royal tutors taught her, she mastered with ease. She could tally the royal treasure on her gold and silver abacus, and charm even the Wizard with her enchantments. In short, she had every gift but love, for in all the kingdom there was no suitable match for her.

So she played the zither and designed great tapestries and trained her finches to eat from her hand, for she had a way with animals.

Jeanne Desy

3 ▶ Key features

The writers

- use vocabulary that suits and gives clues to the type of story they are writing
- give enough background information to set the scene
- introduce the main character within the first few lines

c The Away Team

'Listen,' Damian said fiercely as his team was about to return to the pitch for the second half of the Sunday League match against Kettlesing. 'We can't lose our last home game at the Fold. It'd never be forgotten. It'd be the worst thing possible. So we've got to go out there and get stuck into that lot – and WIN. Nothing else will do. OK?'

Michael Hardcastle

≫
- In text **c**, who exactly is Damian talking to?
- Where does extract **c** take place?
- What type of story would you expect to follow each opening? Choose from these: romance, fairy tale, crime, fantasy, sport story, school story, mystery.

4 ▷ Language skills

Word

Writers give early clues to the type of story they are writing through the **vocabulary** they use. Certain words or phrases are more likely to appear in some types of story than in others.

1 Look at text **a**. These words and phrases suggest that this novel is historical: *hansom cab, dressed in mourning, bonnet, one so fair.*

Write down words or phrases from text a which suggest that this story might be a crime or mystery instead.

2 Make a list of all the words and phrases in text **b** which tell you that it is a fairy tale.

3 List words and phrases from text **c** which have sporting elements.

4 Create your own vocabulary bank of ten words or phrases that you might expect to find in another story type from the list on page 9. For example here is a short list of words for war stories: *flak, bombardment, attack, trench, sapper.*

Spelling

Homophones are words which sound the same or similar, but which have different spellings and meanings:

there – their   son – sun
where – wear

Lee and Alim both wear green baseball caps.

Do you know where they bought them?

5 Find these two words in text **a**: *hansom, mourning*

Write a sentence of your own for each one to show that you understand them.

Their homophone pairs are: *handsome, morning*. Write two more sentences for these words, bringing out the different meanings of the words.

6 Keep a look out for this pair of near homophones: *loose* (text **a**), *lose* (text **c**). These are often confused. Write a sentence for each one to help you learn and remember their meanings.

Sentence

The **semi-colon** (;) is a punctuation mark that can be used to join two main clauses in a sentence. It tells you that the two clauses have something in common, or are close in meaning.

1 Line 9 of text **a** contains this sentence:

> *Her name was Sally Lockhart; and within fifteen minutes, she was going to kill a man.*

Rewrite it as two separate sentences and compare it with the original.

Notice how the original version suggests that she is going to kill a man *because* she is Sally Lockhart. On the other hand, the two separate sentences you have written do not hint that the man's death is linked to her identity.

2 In text **b** the writer could have used a semi-colon before adding her explanation at lines 5 and 6.

> *In short, she had every gift but love; in all the kingdom there was no suitable match for her.*

Notice how the semi-colon replaces the word *for* without changing the link between the two clauses.

Rewrite the final sentence of text **b** using a semi-colon.

Text

The different kinds of story, such as horror, western or fantasy, are called **genres**. Each genre has its own recognisable and typical features.

1 Choose a genre from the list below to match each of the extracts on pages 8–9:

science fiction	adventure
horror	romance
historical	mystery
crime	fantasy
fairy or folk tale	school story
sport story	war

Writers make especially careful choices about the opening paragraphs of a book. There are some useful ways to begin a story, whatever its genre. The writer can introduce the story through **action**, **description** (of the setting or a character) or **dialogue** (conversation).

Sometimes a writer will combine two techniques, but the aim is always to interest readers in the story quickly and encourage them to read on.

2 Which of these three types of introduction is used – action, description or dialogue – for texts **a**, **b** and **c**?

3 Write down one sentence from each text which would encourage you to read on. Compare your choice with that of another student.

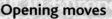

5 ▷ Planning your own writing

❶ Write three story openings. Each one should:

- be no more than three paragraphs long
- be written in a different genre
- introduce the main character

Before you begin to write, make sure you have planned your ideas clearly. You are not going to write the complete stories, but you still need to know how you want each one to end.

▷▷ STARTING POINTS

- crime: a detective arrives at the scene of a crime
- horror: a teenager inherits a mansion from a relative they have never met
- sport: a team captain turns up first at the away ground
- romance: a young man or woman sets off on a singles holiday
- science fiction: a lone pilot docks at an unfamiliar star-port
- fairy tale or fantasy: a prince rides up to a seemingly deserted castle

▷▷ CLUES FOR SUCCESS

- Choose genres that you have read yourself; you will have more ideas to draw on.
- Make a plan. Decide on a main character, a setting and a plot idea.
- Follow the writing frame closely for your first opening. It is based on text a, so you can look back at that to help you.
- Don't try to be too original; copy the features and language of each genre as closely as you can.
- Do not write too much at this stage.

>> WRITING FRAME

On a _____ (weather details) afternoon in _____ (time of year) a _____ (vehicle) drew up outside _____ in _____ (location).

_____ (type of person) got out and _____ (first action we see).

She/He was a person of _____ (age) and _____ (general appearance).

He/She was _____, dressed in _____ with _____ (more physical details or points about how character behaves).

Her/His name was _____; and _____ (a clue as to what might happen in the rest of the story).

>> REDRAFTING AND IMPROVING

Read your three openings with another student. Ask them to identify the genre. They may be able to help with some suggestions to improve your writing.

Now that you have your basic openings, you can vary the sentence structures or add new information and detail. Work on one at a time to do the following:

- Choose one opening in which to concentrate on showing action. What happens to the main character? What are they doing? How are they behaving?

- In the second, concentrate on describing the setting or a character.

- Rewrite the third opening so that your story begins with dialogue. Look back at text **c** for help with this.

- In all three openings keep the vocabulary and content in the style of your chosen genre. Use the word banks you compiled earlier to help you.

- Finally, give a title to each of your openings.

6 > Looking back

- A **genre** is a type of writing which has its own special features. Genre can give clues about the type of story you read.

- A **semi-colon** is sometimes used between two clauses of a sentence; it tells the reader where the two parts have related meanings.

- Stories can open with a piece of **description** or **dialogue**. Another way to begin a story is to launch straight into the **action**.

Meeting people

Purpose

In this unit you will:
- learn about creating and developing fictional characters
- discover how to turn speech into written dialogue
- create and write about convincing characters of your own

➤➤ **Subject links:** *history, media studies, PSHE*

2 **Narrative fiction introducing characters**

Goodnight Mr Tom

'Yes,' said Tom bluntly, on opening the front door. 'What d'you want?'

A harassed middle-aged woman in a green coat and felt hat stood on his step. He glanced at the armband on her sleeve. She gave him an awkward smile.

'I'm the Billeting Officer for this area,' she began.   5

'Oh yes, and what's that got to do wi' me?'

She flushed slightly. 'Well, Mr, Mr…'

'Oakley. Thomas Oakley.'

'Ah, thank you, Mr Oakley.' She paused and took a deep breath. 'Mr Oakley, with the declaration of war imminent…'   10

Tom waved his hand. 'I knows all that. Git to the point. What d'you want?' He noticed a small boy at her side.

'It's him I've come about,' she said. 'I'm on my way to your village hall with the others.'

'What others?'   15

She stepped to one side. Behind the large iron gate which stood at the end of the graveyard were a small group of children. Many of them were filthy and very poorly clad. Only a handful had a blazer or coat. They all looked bewildered and exhausted. One tiny dark-haired girl in the front was hanging firmly on to a new teddy-bear.   20

The woman touched the boy at her side and pushed him forward.

'There's no need to tell me,' said Tom. 'It's obligatory and it's for the war effort.'

'You are entitled to choose your child, I know,' began the woman apologetically.   25

Tom gave a snort.

'But,' she continued, 'his mother wants him to be with someone who's religious or near a church. She was quite adamant. Said she would only let him be evacuated if he was.'

'Was what?' asked Tom impatiently.   30

'Near a church.'

Tom took a second look at the child. The boy was thin and sickly-looking, pale with limp sandy hair and dull grey eyes.

'His name's Willie,' said the woman.

Willie, who had been staring at the ground, looked up. Round his   35
neck, hanging from a piece of string, was a cardboard label. It read
'William Beech'.

Tom was well into his sixties, a healthy, robust, stockily-built man with
a head of thick white hair. Although he was of average height, in Willie's
eyes he was a towering giant with skin like coarse, wrinkled brown paper   40
and a voice like thunder.

He glared at Willie. 'You'd best come in,' he said abruptly.

The woman gave a relieved smile. 'Thank you so much,' she said, and
she backed quickly away and hurried down the tiny path towards the
other children. Willie watched her go.   45

'Come on in,' repeated Tom harshly. 'I ent got all day.'

Michelle Magorian

3 Key features

The writer uses:
- **adjectives** to give basic information about the characters
- **adverbs** to show how the characters behave
- **dialogue** to develop the characters further

- In which period in history is this story set? Explain how you can tell.
- Describe the area in which the story takes place. What clues are there?
- Who is the main character, and how do you know this?

4 Language skills

Word

Adjectives are words which describe somebody or something. They give more information about a noun or pronoun.

① Make a table like this one and complete it with adjectives from the text to describe each character. Note the line numbers in brackets.

Tom	Willie	Billeting Officer
healthy (38)	small (12)	harassed (2)

② We are told at line 28 that Willie's mother 'was quite *adamant*.' Look up the meaning of this adjective in a dictionary or thesaurus. What does it add to your understanding of her and of her son?

③ For each of the adjectives in your table, find a word that could be used in its place. A thesaurus will help you.

Adverbs are words which tell you how something is or how it happens. They give information about verbs. Many adverbs end in *-ly*:

Joe shouted loudly.
Mary complained bitterly.

The extract begins:

Yes, said Tom bluntly...

The adverb tells us how Tom spoke.

④ Find four more adverbs ending in *-ly* in the text. Write down the sentences containing them. Explain what further information they give as in this example:

'Was what?' asked Tom impatiently. The adverb tells me that Tom is losing his temper with the Billeting Officer.

Spelling

A **suffix** is an ending added to a word to produce a new word. You can add the suffix *-ly* to adjectives to create adverbs.

Where words end in a consonant other than *y*, just add *-ly*.

Impatient + ly ➜ *impatiently*

Where words end in *-y*, change the *y* to an *i* and add *-ly*.

Pretty ➜ *Pretti + ly* ➜ *prettily*

Where words end in *-e*, you usually keep the *e* and add *-ly*.

Strange + ly ➜ *strangely*

There are some exceptions such as *duly, truly, wholly*. Look out for and learn them.

Sentence

Speech marks (' ') are used to mark the beginning and end of someone's actual words when a writer adds conversation to the narrative. Speech marks are also called **inverted commas**. They can be written as single inverted commas (' ') or as doubles (" ").

❶ Look carefully at the text lines 5 to 8. It is set out using the rules of direct speech. Make a note of the rules.

> *'I'm the Billeting Officer for this area,' she began.*

- Speech marks go around only the words which are spoken.

- The words which say *who* is speaking are separate and are usually marked off by a comma, before the closing speech marks.

- The full stop comes at the end of the whole sentence.

> *'Oh yes, and what's that got to do wi' me?'*

- If the whole sentence is speech, then the sentence punctuation stays inside the speech marks.

> *She flushed slightly. 'Well, Mr, Mr...'*

- We can learn who is speaking before, after, or even in the middle of the speech, but...

> *'Oakley. Thomas Oakley.'*

- Each time a new speaker begins, the writer must begin a new paragraph, dropping down to the next line of writing.

❷ Write the conversation that would take place between Willie and Tom, once the cottage door closes.

Use correct **direct speech** punctuation.

Text

Dialogue is a conversation. A third of the text is set out as a dialogue. Dialogue brings characters to life. The writer does not tell the reader what to think about them. Instead she shows the people and how they interact.

❶ A good writer will be able to make dialogue sound realistic. She will vary the way that characters speak: sometimes they will use formal language and sometimes colloquial speech.

Formal language is polite and respectful. It can also sound very official or knowledgeable.

Colloquial language is the everyday speech we use and can include local or popular expressions. When it is written down it can give clues to the speaker's **accent** or pronunciation of words.

❷ Which character speaks in careful, formal standard English? Write out one sentence to show this style of speech.

❸ Which character uses **colloquial** English? Write out two phrases in this style of speech.

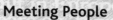

5 ▶ Planning your own writing

1 Using the images on this page, or any of your own, create a character.

- Plan your character in a writing frame like the one opposite. Use note form.

- Write a description of the character.
- Include one paragraph for each of sections 1 to 6 in the frame.
- Give as much information as you can.

STARTING POINTS

- Use the images to suggest what your character is like.
- Base your character on someone you know.
- Spend time people-watching: take detailed notes.
- Combine ideas from all three of the above.
- Be clear about your character's age, background and occupation.

CLUES FOR SUCCESS

- Avoid stereotypes – obvious kinds of people. The best characters have something out of the ordinary.
- Don't make your character all good or all bad.
- Give him or her a goal or an ambition.
- Create some friends, family and enemies for him or her. Relationships are important.
- Choose your character's name very carefully. Names can say a lot.

WRITING FRAME

1 Name:
   Age:
   Physical appearance:
   Clothing likes and dislikes:

2 Occupation:
   Hobbies:

3 Special talents:
   Likes and dislikes:
   Things they find difficult to do:

4 Close friends or relatives:
   Enemies:

5 Goal or ambition in life:

6 Why is it important to achieve
   that goal? What is there to lose?

REDRAFTING AND IMPROVING

Share your description with another student and find out about the character they have created. To develop your writing further you can use your own character and the one created by the other person. Write about a time when they meet. Use your own ideas for the encounter, or choose from this list.

Your characters could meet:

- on the first day at a new school
- on holiday
- in a hospital waiting area
- through a chat room
- when one of them is wrongly accused of shop-lifting

- Use your character descriptions as a starting point only.
- Include only a small amount of physical description, to give the reader a picture.
- Concentrate on the dialogue between the two characters.
- Develop what the reader learns about the characters by showing their actions and reactions to others.

6 Looking back

- **Adjectives** describe people or things and give helpful information about a noun or pronoun. In fiction they are important for building up vivid characters and settings.

- **Adverbs** are words which tell you how something is or how it happens. Like adjectives, they help add detail to stories.

- **Dialogue** is a conversation. It brings characters to life. When you write dialogue in your own stories, always check the rules of speech punctuation.

Shakespeare's imaginary forces

1 ▶ Purpose

In this unit you will:

- discover how Shakespeare captures the imagination of an audience
- read speeches aloud, thinking about the impact on the listener
- prepare your own vivid commentary of an event

▶▶ **Subject links:** *drama, history, media studies*

2 ▶ A speech from a Shakespeare play

Prologue to The Life of King Henry V

The play tells the story of the young King Henry who, believing that the throne of France is rightfully his, sets out to win it in battle with the French. Shakespeare emphasises Henry's good qualities throughout the play: he is kind and fair to the people he conquers, liked by all his soldiers and wins the hand of the French princess along with the crown.

The climax of the play is the Battle of Agincourt, which took place in 1415. Though greatly outnumbered by French forces, Henry's army still win the day.

At the start of Act I of the play, the Chorus speaks these words.

ENTER CHORUS.

CHORUS	**O for** a Muse of fire, that would ascend	*if only I had…*
	The brightest heaven of **invention**;	*fantasy, imagination*
	A kingdom for a stage, princes to act	
	And monarchs to behold the swelling scene.	
5	Then should the war-like **Harry**, like himself,	*King Henry V*
	Assume the **port** of Mars; and at his heels,	*appearance*
	Leash'd in like hounds, should famine, sword, and fire	

	Crouch for employment. But pardon, **gentles** all,	*gentlemen*
	The flat **unraised** spirits that hath dar'd	*lifeless*
10	On this unworthy **scaffold** to bring forth	*the stage*
	So great an object: can this **cockpit** hold	*arena for cockfights*
	The **vasty** fields of France? or may we cram	*huge*
	Within this wooden O the very **casques**	*helmets*
	That did **affright** the air at **Agincourt**?	*startle; battle of 1415*
15	O, pardon! since a **crooked figure** may	*written symbol (M)*
	Attest in little place a million;	*represent, stand for*
	And let us, **ciphers** to this great **accompt**,	*zeros; account*
	On your imaginary forces work.	
	Suppose within the girdle of these walls	
20	Are now confin'd two mighty **monarchies**,	*powers, kingdoms*
	Whose high upreared and **abutting** fronts	*facing each other*
	The perilous narrow ocean parts asunder:	
	Piece out our imperfections with your thoughts:	*fill in what we miss*
	Into a thousand parts divide one man,	
25	And make imaginary **puissance**;	*power*
	Think when we talk of horses that you see them	
	Printing their proud hoofs i' the receiving earth;	
	For 'tis your thoughts that now must **deck** our kings,	*dress up*
	Carry them here and there, jumping o'er times,	
30	Turning the accomplishment of many years	
	Into an hour-glass: for the which supply,	
	Admit me Chorus to this history;	*let me act as*
	Who **prologue**-like your humble patience pray,	*introduction*
34	Gently to hear, kindly to judge, our play. *[Exit]*	

William Shakespeare

3 > Key features

The writer:

- supplies detailed and vivid descriptions by using carefully-chosen **diction**
- involves and directs the audience using **imperative sentences**
- writes in poetic form, using **blank verse** and **rhyming couplets**

>>
- What does the Chorus tell us will be needed in the first eight lines of the speech?
- What must the audience add to the performance? (lines 19–31)
- What will the Chorus and actors supply? (lines 31–32)

4 > Language skills

Word

Diction is the name given to a writer's choice of vocabulary. Shakespeare's diction creates striking images. At the time when he was writing, very little scenery and few props were used on stage and many actors wore everyday dress. Because of this, dramatists found ways of helping the audience to picture the scenes and action more vividly.

1 In Act I lines 6–8, the terrible destructions that war brings – famine, sword and fire – are likened to dogs of war. Write down other words or phrases from the speech which make you think of battles or conflict.

2 In the speech, what are these things compared to:
the theatre building? (lines 11–14)
the king himself? (lines 5–6)

Who or what were:
the Muses? (line 1)
Mars? (line 6)

Find out about them using an encyclopaedia or dictionary of phrase and fable. Write a description or explanation of them in your own words, and explain why they help the audience to visualise the scene and the king himself.

Spelling

Words that contain the vowel combination -ou- have two main pronunciation sounds:

-ou- sounded as 'ow':
hounds, crouch, out

-ou- sounded as 'or':
Agincourt, your

-ou- is pronounced differently in words like *should* and *perilous*.

1 List four more words from the speech with -ou- pronounced 'ow'.

2 Find one more example from the speech of -ou- pronounced 'or'.

Sentence

Imperative sentences are ones which tell you or ask you to do something. They may be direct orders:

Carry them here and there! (line 29)

1 Make a list of every imperative sentence giving a direct order that the Chorus uses in the speech. To start you off:

Piece out…
Suppose…

Simple, imperative sentences, like the ones you have listed, begin with a verb.

2 Underline the verb in each sentence on your list.

3 Using the list of imperative verbs you have made, explain in your own words what the Chorus asks the audience to do.

Text

Blank verse is a form of poetry which uses lines of regular length and similar rhythm.

Shakespeare's plays are written mostly as poetry. The most common form of poetry found in his plays is blank verse. It is a form which helps to create the impression of natural speech.

1 Practise reading the speech aloud. Avoid the temptation to stop at the end of each line. Instead, notice where the punctuation invites you to breathe or pause – at commas, semi-colons and full stops. Look out for the sense or meaning of each sentence.

Record your performance of the speech and listen to it. Repeat the recording as many times as you wish, aiming to get the important points across.

Rhyming couplets are two consecutive lines of poetry that rhyme. You will find a rhyming couplet at the end of the speech. After this the action of the play begins.

You probably already know that in Shakespeare's day, actors performed in broad daylight. The lights did not dim or go out at the end of each scene; no curtain fell and often there was nothing visual to show a scene change.

2 Why do you think Shakespeare changes the verse pattern from blank verse to a rhyming couplet at this point?

5 ▸ Planning your own writing

1 Write a radio commentary of an exciting event, aiming to convey vivid details about the scene and the action to your listener.

- The event may be real or imaginary, recent or historical.

- Concentrate on events.

- Tell them from only one point of view.

- Remember that your listener cannot see what was happening. You must act as their eyes. Your descriptions must be straightforward and crystal clear.

▸▸ **STARTING POINTS**

- A sporting event – last Saturday's school fixture, your local or national team's latest match...

- A public event – a local celebration, street carnival, Mayor's parade...

- A historical event – a battle, royal wedding...

- A private occasion – great-grandpa's 100th birthday, sister's dance display...

- A funny occasion – packing the car for a camping holiday, first few minutes of the January sale at a local store, a supermarket shopping trip...

▸▸ **CLUES FOR SUCCESS**

- Set the scene clearly.

- Mention your main 'players' near the start of your commentary.

- Tell the events from one angle, as if you are watching from a single spot.

- Set out the events in strict chronological order – from start to finish – emphasising the highlights.

- End with a dramatic moment, an arrival, an achievement or a completion.

- Use the steps below to organise your ideas.

- Use the suggested phrases or invent your own.

WRITING FRAME

1 What is the event?

2 Set the scene.

3 Who are the main players? Describe what the players were wearing, how they seemed to be feeling, their gestures to the crowd, etc.

4 Continue narrating the events as they happened.

5 Work on your listeners' imaginations using imperative sentences

6 Give a clear end-point.

7 A final comment?

'There was a fine turnout for today's
....'

'Spectators lined the .... and were in .... mood.'

'First to appear was ....'
'Within minutes ....'

'Halfway through ....'
'Imagine ....'

'Picture the scene ....'

'At the final ....'
'A spokesperson said ....'
'The manager had this to say ....'

REDRAFTING AND IMPROVING

Here you can change and add details to your commentary.

- Find out how vivid your account of the event is by reading aloud to someone. Ask them which parts of the commentary they found hard to follow. They may suggest that you add or change information to help them picture the scene or action.

- Sharpen your diction, replacing everyday phrases with more precise and evocative words.

- You could end your commentary with a rhyming couplet. Commentators have been known to do this!

6 › Looking back

- A writer's **diction**, or choice of words, helps create particular images, ideas, impressions or moods.

- An **imperative sentence** is a command or call for action. It may be a direct order or, worded more persuasively, a request.

- Two consecutive lines of poetry that rhyme are known as **rhyming couplets**. Shakespeare uses a couplet at the end of every scene to let the audience know that the scene or time is about to change.

Picture this

Purpose

In this unit you will:

- find out about Mind Maps® and their uses
- discover how to select and make useful notes
- practise this note-making technique

Subject links: *history, subjects which use note-taking or problem-solving techniques*

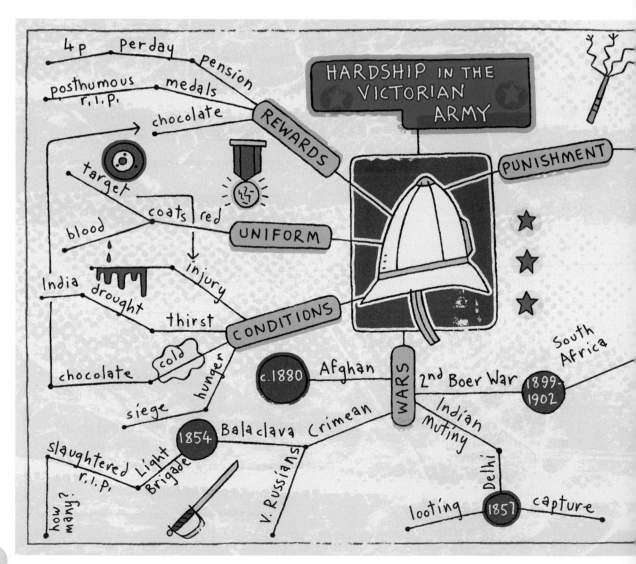

2 > A Mind Map® based on an information text

Notes on the hardship faced by soldiers in the Victorian army

You may have come across Mind Maps before. They can be used for different purposes:

- *for notes to record something*
- *for notes from a discussion or brainstorm*
- *to explore your own thoughts about something*

A student was asked to explore the topic of hardship in the army in Victorian times. He drew the diagram below in a Mind Map style after reading Terry Deary's The Vile Victorians. *He made his notes look like this:*

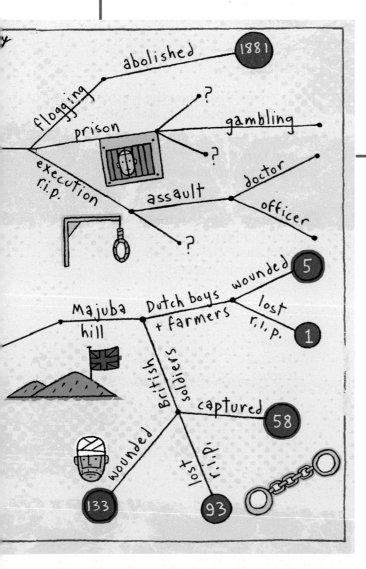

Once you have made a Mind Map you can use it to:

- *organise your ideas before writing*
- *plan a speech*
- *prompt you when making a speech*
- *make revision notes*

3 > Key features

The writer

- places the topic at the centre of the page
- uses only key words to note each idea or fact
- includes symbols or graphics

- What was the disadvantage of a wearing a red jacket as uniform?
- At which battle were 133 British army soldiers wounded?
- When was flogging finally banned as a punishment for soldiers?

4 Language skills

Word

A **noun** is a word that names an object or a feeling. Most of the key words in a Mind Map, or any form of note-taking will be nouns.

There are four main types of noun:

common nouns: they name everyday things: *man, dog, farmer, uniform*

proper nouns: they name specific people or things and always begin with a capital letter: *Peter, Thames, Russia, Delhi*

collective nouns: they name a group of people or things: *crowd, flock, army*

abstract nouns: they name ideas or concepts: *love, war, hunger*

1 From the Mind Map, write down three common nouns which tell you the rewards that soldiers received.

2 Find three proper nouns which name wars or battles.

3 Find a collective noun for *cavalry soldiers*.

4 Write down three abstract nouns which name conditions suffered by the soldiers.

Most of the key words in any note-form will be nouns, but not all. Sometimes **verbs**, words which name an action or state, and **adjectives**, which describe a noun, need to be noted down.

5 At the end of the Battle of Majuba Hill some of the British soldiers survived. Write down the three verbs which tell you what happened to the ones who didn't survive.

6 Find the adjective which describes the soldiers' coats.
What else does it describe in the diagram?

Spelling

Many nouns that name the jobs or activities that people do, end with either *-er* or *-or*:

soldier, farmer, officer
actor, doctor, councillor

1 List and complete the following nouns using the correct ending in each case. Use a dictionary to check your answers.

read____
supervis____
ment____
speak____
writ____
teach____
execut____
football____
explor____
capt____

Sentence

A **sentence** is a piece of language which makes sense on its own. It begins with a capital letter and ends with a full stop, question mark or exclamation mark.

Single nouns, verbs, adjectives or phrases do not usually mean much alone.

Each branch of the Mind Map can be written as a sentence by adding other linking words.

could become

Some of the rewards *a soldier could receive were* medals, *although many were* awarded *posthumously – after they died.*

1 Create sentences using the information from these branches. Hint: move out from the centre of the Mind Map.

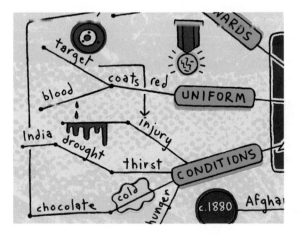

Text

The art of putting images and lettering together is called **graphics**. Graphics can help to highlight or link together ideas in a text. They are often used in note taking.

They can be:
arrows
symbols
pictures
shapes
different
colour codes.

Graphics are also helpful when revising notes for tests because they are memory aids.

1 On the Mind Map, what symbol is used by the writer to show that he needs to find out more information on a topic?

2 Make a key to each of the graphics in the Mind Map. Draw each symbol and add an explanation of what it shows.

3 Add to the key any graphics that you use when making your own notes. Or invent some symbols to use in the future. For instance, what would you use as a graphic short-cut to show:

a marriage
a birth
a victory
a shipwreck?

5 > Planning your own writing

1 Draw up your own Mind Map, making notes from the **Starting point** text. The topic for your notes is *Conditions in Victorian schools*.

>> CLUES FOR SUCCESS

- Use plain paper in **landscape** format – with the long edge across the top.

- Start with your heading in the centre of the page. Draw a picture around it.

- For each new idea or topic start a new branch of the tree.

- Use keywords (mostly nouns, with a few verbs or adjectives).

- Use only one word for each line on the branch.

- Use graphics – arrows, colour, pictures and symbols – to make links or to highlight important areas.

>> STARTING POINT

In 1870 the Education Bill was passed.

Some vile Victorian teachers didn't believe in talking to pupils to find out why they did something wrong. They simply punished them.

5   Punishments included kneeling on hard floor-boards for twenty minutes, the strap and the cane.

Teachers could train by working in the classroom with an older teacher. Trainee teachers started at the age of 14. At one men's college the trainee teachers could not leave the college except at certain times, not go to the bedrooms during the day, not stay up after 10.00 p.m., not have a light on in their bedroom, not go to any public house, not smoke, not
10   make friends with the local people and they had to take some form of active exercise every afternoon!

The Victorians believed that boys should be treated differently from girls...and that men were more important than women. This showed in the schools. In 1870, women teachers were paid 58 pounds a year...but men were paid 94!

15   Boys' lessons included carpentry, farmwork, gardening, shoe making, drawing, handicrafts. Girls' lessons included housewifery (sweeping, dusting, making beds and bathing a baby), needlework and cookery.

Lessons were often just learning things by heart, then repeating them.

There were often as many as 70 or 80 pupils in one class. The teachers would have to shout
20   or even scream to be heard above the noise of the children.

Terry Deary (adapted)

>> WRITING FRAME

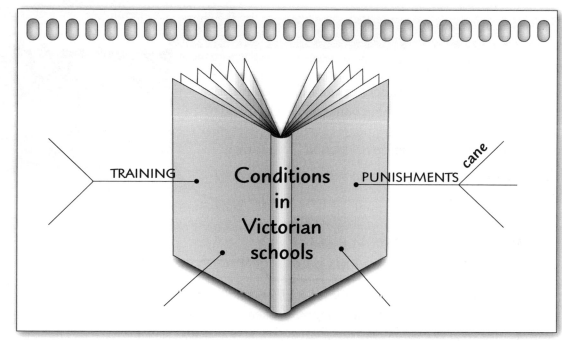

TRAINING

Conditions in Victorian schools

PUNISHMENTS

cane

>> REDRAFTING AND IMPROVING

1 As soon as you finish your Mind Map, put it to one side.

2 Read the **Starting point** text again. Turn it over.

3 Add any further notes to your map without going back to the text.

4 Still without looking back at the text, write a summary of what you have read. Call it *Conditions in Victorian Schools* and use only the notes in your Mind Map to remind you. Write in paragraphs, using a new topic for each one. The sentences will come from each of the branches.

6 > Looking back

- A **noun** is a word that names an object or a feeling. Most of the key words in a Mind Map are **nouns**.

- **Graphics** combine letters and images. They can emphasise or link together ideas in a text.

Huddle up!

In this unit you will:
- read about how a student explored a scientific idea
- see how writing can help you explore ideas and develop your thinking
- plan and describe an investigation of your own

>> **Subject links:** *science, mathematics, CDT, geography*

2 **An investigation report**

Percy the penguin and his pals

Some students watched a film about how penguins survive in extremely cold climates. They were asked to investigate the ways to prevent heat loss from bodies. One student examined why penguins huddle together for warmth.

Introduction

I intend to find out whether huddling together in groups keeps penguins warmer than standing alone.

Several factors affect a penguin's body temperature. They are:
- the penguin's diet
- whether it is wet or dry
- if it is active
- its body size/weight
- its natural insulation
- whether it is huddling with other penguins.

The first three factors are hard to simulate in the lab.

Prediction

I predict that keeping warm in a group will be more effective. If you stand alone, you lose heat from all of the surface area of your body which is exposed to the cold air. (a) If one surface of your body is in contact with someone else, then the heat from both of your bodies will not escape so quickly.

If several penguins stand close together, then less of their body surface will be exposed to the air; therefore keeping more heat between them. (b)

If a large group of penguins stand together, some will have no surfaces (other than on the tops of their heads). They will be warmer. (c)

Planning

Equipment needed:
- test tubes, tongs and claws to hold them upright
- elastic bands to group tubes together
- kettle to boil water for test tubes
- bungs and thermometers
-        stop-clock

How will I make sure that all the tubes (penguins) start at the same temperature?
Pour boiling water into tubes and start stop-clock only when they get to 80°C.

How will I make sure that the surface area of all penguins is the same?
Use all the same sized tubes, all of the same material.

How will I make sure that I am measuring the same rate of heat loss for each experiment I try?
Keep to a time interval. I will measure temperature every 30 seconds for 5 minutes.

How will I find out different rates of heat loss?
Experiment 1 – single penguin
Experiment 2 – 3 penguins
Experiment 3 – 7 penguins – using two measurements: one for a penguin on the outside of the huddle and one for the penguin in the centre.

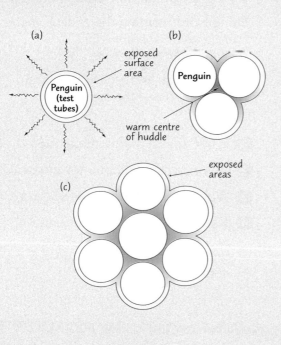

3 > Key features

The writer
- uses scientific vocabulary to describe and record events
- uses questions and answers to explore possibilities
- presents information with sub-headings, bullet points, diagrams and other layout features

- Why can't the first three factors (lines 6–8) be tested by the student?
- What will happen to the 'penguin' placed at the centre of Experiment 3?

33

4 Language skills

Word

Scientific vocabulary is helpful when you want to record, report or describe something very accurately.

The writer describes her ideas, plans and actions very carefully. She tells us that she is going to *examine*, *investigate* and *simulate*.

1 Write down the exact meanings of each of these three words.

At the start of her investigation, the writer says:
I predict that keeping warm in a group will be more effective.
She uses the verb to predict in the present tense – *I predict*.

One section of her investigation report has the heading **Prediction**. This is the noun form of the word *predict*. Notice the *-tion* ending.

2 For each of these present tense words, write out the past tense (using *-ed*) and the noun form (using *-tion*). The first one is done for you.
simulate, simulated, simulation
observe
investigate
examine
experiment
assume

Spelling

Metre or *meter* – what's the difference?

Metre is the British English spelling for the word which means 100 centimetres. It can also mean the rhythm of lines of poetry, measured by the number of syllables.

The American English spelling is *meter*.

In Britain we write millimetre, centimetre, kilometre, etc. when we are talking about measurements of length.

Some words contain the ending *-meter*: *thermometer, anemometer, speedometer, tachometer*.

In both British and American English these are written the same.

1 What does a thermometer measure?

2 What does a tachometer measure?

3 What does a barometer measure?

4 Name five more instruments which end in *-meter*? List them, with those above, and write a sentence for each one.

Sentence

Many sentences are made up of a main clause and one or more **subordinate clauses**. A subordinate clause is one that adds information or meaning to the main clause. When we explore and develop ideas we often use sentences with subordinate clauses, like this one:

If you stand alone, all of the surface area of your body is exposed to the cold air.

1 Write out these sentences and underline the subordinate clause.

If a large group of penguins stand together, then some will have no surfaces exposed to the outside.

If several penguins stand close together, then less of their body surface will be exposed to the air.

The heat from your body will not escape so quickly if you are in physical contact with another person.

2 Make up four sentences with subordinate clauses. Use the formula *if x happens...y will happen* as your pattern:

If I don't go to school tomorrow, I won't have to do my science test.

If is one word which can be used to link subordinate clauses to the main clause of the sentence. Other words that do this are: *because, although, since.*

Text

The layout of a factual text might include any or all of these features:

sub-headings	*diagrams*
charts	*graphs*
bullet points	*numbering*
boxes	*shading*

They can be used to give visual interest and help the reader follow the text. They can also be short-cuts: a graph gives instant visual information which would take many more words of prose to explain.

1 Which of the layout features in the list above can you find in the text? Say which ones are used to give visual interest. Which ones are short-cuts?

35

5 ▸ Planning your own writing

Plan, perform and describe an investigation. Use an idea of your own, or select from the suggestions in **Starting points** below.

1 Your investigation can be scientific or mathematical, or it can be a CDT or food technology project.

2 Before you carry out any investigation, be sure to check with your teacher that what you plan to do is SAFE.

3 Predict what you think will happen and plan to test your theory. Make diagrams to show your methods or your thinking.

▸▸ CLUES FOR SUCCESS

- First decide on the things which will affect your investigation: these are called factors. Look back at the text to see how this is done, or ask a teacher to help.

- Choose just one factor for your investigation. Be practical – you must be able to test it in the lab or at home without too much equipment.

- Plan your investigation. Ask questions and suggest answers.

▸▸ STARTING POINTS

- How could you make sugar dissolve in water faster?

- What affects the size of a shadow?

- Can magnets be stopped? Can magnets be made?

- Can animals hear underwater?

- If you want to know where a sound is coming from, is it better to have one ear or two?

▸▸ REDRAFTING AND IMPROVING

Have you included:

- a prediction, using *if x happens... y will happen* sentences to explore the possibilities (See the **Sentence** section on page 35.)

- an explanation of what you need to make your tests fair, in question and answer form

Have you presented your report in the most useful layout using:

- sub-headings
- bullet points or numbering
- diagrams
- charts
- shading

>> **WRITING FRAME**

Use these headings as part of your layout.

TITLE OF INVESTIGATION

Introduction

1 In one sentence write down what you are going to do in the investigation: *I intend to find out...*

2 Write down a list of things which could be changed in the experiment — factors. Use bullet points to set them out.

3 Choose one factor — the variable — to investigate: *I chose to examine the huddling technique.*

Prediction

Guess what will happen in your experiments. Make sure you give explanations to support your theories: *I predict that if I double the amount of light, the rate of photosynthesis will also double.*

Use some of these constructions to help you: *this is because..., however..., if ..., therefore..., in this case....*

Planning

1 List all equipment and ingredients/materials.

2 Describe the method you will use. If someone else wanted to do this investigation, they should be able to follow this.

3 The test should be 'fair'. Use a question and answer format to show that it is: How will I make sure that all the tubes start at the same temperature? Pour boiling water into tubes and start stop-clock only when they get to 80°C.

6 ▷ Looking back

- **Scientific vocabulary** records, reports or describes observations and events with precision. It helps other scientists repeat and check the results of experiments.

- The **layout** of a text can include different graphic or visual features: such as sub-headings, diagrams or shading. They provide extra information in the text.

- **Question and answer technique** is a way of exploring and developing ideas. It can be used in speech or writing.

Razor-sharp arguments

1 ▷ **Purpose**

In this unit you will:
- read a piece by a modern philosopher
- learn how to explore ideas
- write your own discussion and solution

▶▶ **Subject links:** *science, maths, thinking skills*

2 ▷ **A discussion text**

'Ockham's razor' from *The Philosophy Files*

Most people will tell you that philosophy is a difficult and complicated subject. However, it is not always as tricky as you would expect! One famous medieval philosopher called William of Ockham (1287–1347) came to this conclusion: when you have two theories, or hypotheses, it is always best to choose the simplest explanation. (Surprisingly, you might think, other philosophers have not always agreed with him.) Here is how a modern philosopher explains the principle which is known as Ockham's razor.

There is a famous philosophical principle which says that when you are presented with two hypotheses both of which are otherwise equally supported by the evidence, it is always reasonable to

5 believe the *simpler* hypothesis. This principle is called *Ockham's razor*. It seems a very plausible principle.

Here's an illustration of how Ockham's razor works. Suppose you are shown a box with a button on the side and a light bulb on top. You

10 see that, whenever the button is pressed, the light

comes on. Otherwise the light stays off. Now let's look at two competing hypotheses, both of which explain what you see.

15 The first hypothesis is that the button and the bulb are linked by a circuit to a battery *inside* the box. Press the button and the circuit is completed. That lights up the bulb.

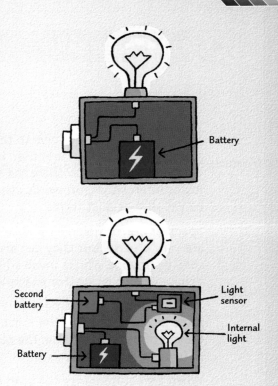

Battery

The second hypothesis is more complicated.
It says that the button is attached to an
20 electrical circuit linking a battery to a second light bulb inside the box. When the button is pressed, this internal light bulb comes on. A light-sensor inside the box then detects this and connects a *second* electrical
25 circuit linking a *second* battery to the bulb you see on the outside of the box. That lights up the outside bulb.

Second battery

Light sensor

Internal light

Battery

Now, which of these two hypotheses is more reasonable, do you think? True, both hypotheses are
30 equally consistent with what you have seen: on both hypotheses the light will come on when and only when you press the button. But it seems wrong to say that both hypotheses are equally *reasonable*. Surely it is more reasonable to believe the first hypothesis than
35 it is to believe the second, because the second hypothesis is less simple: it says there are two electrical circuits in the box, not one.

Steven Law

3 ▷ Key features

The writer
- uses some specialist terms
- uses both active and passive sentences
- uses paragraphs to structure the discussion

≫ ● How many bulbs and batteries are needed for the first hypothesis?
● How many electrical circuits are needed for the second hypothesis?
● Which of the two explanations would you choose?

4 > Language skills

Word

Jargon is the name we give to the special words and phrases used by groups of people who share the same job or interest. Jargon words can also be called specialist terms.

Specialist terms used by philosophers are very precise, but they can also be used by anyone who is involved in a debate or discussion. For example:

A *hypothesis* is a statement. It is meant to be put to a test, so that it can be proved to be true or false. The plural of *hypothesis* is *hypotheses*.

When two statements can both be true, they are *consistent*.

A belief is *reasonable* when held by someone whose only interest is in finding out the truth.

1 Write out the two hypotheses from the text.

> *The first hypothesis is that...*
> *The second hypothesis says that...*

Persuader words like *surely*, *obviously* and *clearly* are used in discussions and debates when the writer or speaker wants to persuade you of the truth of what they are saying.

2 Find the persuader word in the final paragraph of the text. What is the writer asking you to believe?

Spelling

Negative prefixes change the meaning of a word to its opposite. *Disagree* is formed by adding the prefix *dis-* to the root word *agree*. *Dis-* is called a negative prefix. Other negative prefixes are: *un- im- in-* and *il-*.

When you add a negative prefix, you do not change the spelling of the original word.

1 Add a negative prefix to each of these words. Then check with a dictionary that you have used the correct prefix with each word.

> *reasonable, plausible, consistent, logical, correct, complicated, believe, probable*

Sentence

In an **active sentence** someone carries out an action.

Press the button.

In this active sentence someone (you) does the pressing.

In a **passive sentence** the action happens to someone or something.

When the button is pressed the light comes on.

In this passive sentence the button does nothing, but something happens to it (it is pressed). Debaters often use passive sentences because they sound less personal and one-sided.

1 Here are three active sentences. Change them to passive sentences by changing the order of the subject and object and altering the verb. The first one is done for you.

Lucy fed the cat.
The cat was fed by Lucy.

The cat ate the food.

Lucy's mum washed the bowl.

2 Now change these three sentences from passive to active.

Frank was run over by a bus.

He was rushed to hospital by ambulance.

Fortunately he was patched up by the doctors.

Text

The **structure** of a text is the way it is put together in paragraphs. When you write a discussion text such as this one, you would usually use a particular structure.

First explain the issue or idea in one or two paragraphs. State what it is you are setting out to test or challenge.

Second, set out the hypotheses or theories. Give evidence for them. In this text there are only two theories to examine. The writer uses a different paragraph for each one.

Finally in the last paragraph, question or discuss the findings. You may give an opinion about which hypothesis is correct, or you may invite the reader to decide.

1 Go back to the text and read each paragraph carefully. Then write out (in full) one sentence from each paragraph which sums up the key point.

5 ▶ Planning your own writing

The truth is out there! Find it using the Ockham's razor principle. Solve a mystery and write out your discussion of it.

1 Decide on a topic that needs an explanation. Pick something that has always puzzled you or use one from the **Starting points**.

2 Offer two competing explanations: these will be your hypotheses.

3 Show which explanation is simpler.

4 Believe the simpler one!

▶ STARTING POINTS

- There has never been a newspaper report about the President of the USA holding a summit meeting with aliens. Why is this?

- Anne and Bill have never met. Today they sit next to each other on a plane and find they have something in common. How can this have happened?

- The only evidence that scientists have for the Loch Ness monster is from photographs. Does the creature exist?

- Ships and aircraft which go missing over the Bermuda Triangle never leave any visible wreckage on the sea. Why?

- President Kennedy was undoubtedly assassinated. Was his killer really a lone gunman, or was there a conspiracy?

▶ CLUES FOR SUCCESS

- Give as much background detail to the topic as you can, before you set up the hypotheses.

- Sometimes when you are discussing ideas there will be several different reasons or hypotheses that spring to mind. For the purpose of this exercise, use only two opposing explanations.

- Use persuader words to point your reader towards the answer.

- Both of your hypotheses may seem reasonable, so remember to choose the simpler one!

▶ REDRAFTING AND IMPROVING

- Check the structure of your writing. Have you dealt with each of the two hypotheses and their evidence in separate paragraphs?

- Have you introduced a persuader word to convince your reader of the solution to the problem?

- Check that you have used specialist terms correctly.

- Try out your hypotheses on a friend. If they are not convinced, ask them to form a new hypothesis of their own.

≫ WRITING FRAME

Paragraph 1:
Set out the topic for discussions with as much detail as you can.

> Imagine that you are with me on holiday in Egypt. We are visiting the pyramids. You marvel at their size and wonder how they were built. I wonder too, but I wonder why they were built.

Paragraph 2:
State your first hypothesis.

> One theory says that the pyramids are the most magnificent tombs for the pharaohs...

Give as much evidence as you can.

> Chambers inside the pyramids, long-since looted, were said to hold great treasures...

Paragraph 3:
Outline your second, opposing hypothesis in the same way as you did the first.

> Others take a different view, claiming that the pyramids are actually huge astronomical maps of the universe...

Paragraph 4:
Come to a decision about your hypotheses.

> Obviously it is not plausible that the pharaohs...

Alternatively give your reader some clues, using persuader words, before you offer them the chance to make up their own mind.

> It seems that the simplest argument... But which one is really true?

6 ▷ Looking back

- **Jargon** is used by people who share the same job or interest. Jargon words can also be called **specialist terms**. They usually have very precise meanings.

- **Active and passive sentences** make a difference to how we understand what is happening in a text. In an **active sentence** someone carries out an action. In a **passive sentence** the action happens *to* someone or something.

- The **structure** of a text is the way it is put together in paragraphs. Different types of text need different structures.

Stories to share

Purpose

In this unit you will:

- read and compare three texts written for very young children
- discover how writers make books appeal to children, even if they can't read yet
- write a short story for a child under the age of six

▶▶ **Subject links:** *art, PSHE, media studies*

2 **Picture book stories**

Three stories for under-fives

If you ever have to babysit for a small child, you may discover how picture books can keep even the tiniest baby amused and interested. Here are some examples.

a When we went to the park

When Grandpa and I put on our coats and went to the park...
We saw one black cat sitting on a wall,
   Two big girls licking ice-creams,
Three ladies chatting on a bench,
   Four babies in buggies,
Five children playing in the sandpit,
   Six runners running,
Seven dogs chasing one another,
   Eight boys kicking a ball,
Nine ducks swimming on the pond,
   Ten birds swooping in the sky,
And so many leaves that I couldn't count them all.
   On the way back we saw the black cat again.
Then we went home for tea.

Shirley Hughes

b This is the bear

This is the bear who fell in the bin.
This is the dog who pushed him in.
This is the man who picked up the sack.
This is the driver who would not come back.
This is the bear who went to the dump
  and fell on the pile with a bit of a bump.
This is the boy who took the bus
  and went to the dump to make a fuss.
This is the man in an awful grump who searched ...

Sarah Hayes

c Quacky quack-quack!

This little baby had some bread;
His mummy gave it to him for the ducks,
  but he started eating it instead.
Lots of little ducky things came
  swimming along,
Thinking it was feeding time,
  but they were wrong!
The baby held on to the bag,
  he wouldn't let go;
And the crowd of noisy ducky birds
  started to grow.
They made a lot of ducky noises...
  quacky quack-quack!

Then a whole load of geese swam up
  and went *honk! honk!* at the back.
And when a band went marching by,
  in gold and red and black,
Nobody could hear the tune – all they
  could hear was... *honk! honk!*
Quacky quack-quack!
'Louder, boys,' said the bandmaster,
  'give it a bit more puff.'
So the band went *toot! toot!* ever so
  loud, but it still wasn't enough.
Then all over the city, including the city zoo,
All the animals heard the noise and started
  making noises too.
All the donkeys went... *ee-aw! ee-aw!*
All the dogs went...

Ian Whybrow

3 ❭ Key features

The writers:
- use simple vocabulary
- use sentences which are easy to follow
- encourage the child to take part in the storytelling

❯❯
- Which useful everyday pattern could a child learn from 'When we went to the park?'
- Which words and phrases in *This is the bear* might help a child just beginning to read?
- At which points in *Quacky quack-quack!* would the child join in with the reader of the story?

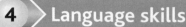

4 Language skills

Word

When a word has a sound which echoes its meaning, such as *smack* or *clap*, we call this **onomatopoeia**.

1 The word *bump* in line 6 of *This is the bear* is one example of onomatopoeia. Make a list of the examples of onomatopoeia in *Quacky quack-quack!*

2 Collect as many examples of onomatopoeia as you can, that describe the sounds made by animals or musical instruments.

3 Continue your list with other sounds, such as the noises made by machinery. Keep your lists safe for later activities.

Spelling

Adding the **suffix** *-ing* to a verb can be very simple:

lick ➜ licking
play ➜ playing

1 Add -ing to these verbs: *swoop, eat, kick, think, march*

If the verb ends in -e, as in *chase*, drop the final -e, then add -ing:

chase   chas + ing ➜ chasing
make   mak + ing ➜ making

2 Add -ing to these verbs: *write, illustrate, rhyme*

Sentence

A **simple sentence** contains only one clause:

I put on my coat.

Compound sentences have two or more clauses. The clauses are joined by **conjunctions**, linking words like *and, but* or *so*:

I put on my coat and *went to the park.*

1 Each pair of simple sentences below can be joined together with conjunctions. Make each pair into one compound sentence and write it out in full.

The bread was for the ducks.
He began to eat it himself.

The ball fell in the sandpit.
The children threw it out.

Sometimes writers add more information to sentences by using clauses which begin with: *who, which* or *whom*:

This is the bear who fell in the bin.

2 Add some extra information to each of the sentences below using a *wh-* word.

The bear, who was pushed by the dog, fell into the bin.

The dogs _____ ran right out of the park.

The cat _____ licked its paw.

The band _____ marched past.

The book _____ was a very good read.

The baby _____ sat in its buggy.

Text

A story for a child must always have a very simple **plot** or storyline.

Lists are often used in children's books as a simple form of plot. In *When we went to the park* the list of numbers from 1 to 10 is used in this way. For each number, a new detail is added to the story.

A simple plot usually has:

- an opening
- some details which develop the story
- a tricky moment or a problem to solve
- a happy ending

1 Look at *When we went to the park*. Line 1 is the opening and line 14 gives a happy ending. Which lines develop the story?

Children's writers often use **rhyme**, **rhythm** and **repetition** to help toddlers join in with the story. The patterns in the language help them to enjoy the words and sounds.

Words ending with the same (or similar) sounds are said to **rhyme**.

> *ago – know*
> *few – dew*
> *along– wrong*

Rhymes help the child join in. Even if she cannot read, she can guess the rhyme word.

2 Read all three texts out loud to get a sense of the sounds and patterns in the words.

3 How many of the texts contain rhyme? Which one has most rhyme?

Rhythm is like the beat in music. It helps carry the reader and child along.

4 Which text do you think has the best rhythm? Explain to another student why you like this rhythm and how it helps the story.

Repetition is where words, phrases or whole sentences are repeated. Children's stories use lots of repetition. The child learns the pattern and joins in each time it appears.

5 For each text, write down the words which the toddler might find easy to join in with.

5 ▷ Planning your own writing

Write a story for a child under the age of six.

- Keep it short: no more than 150 words.
- The child should be able to join in with the story.
- Use your own idea for a plot or use one of the **Starting points**.

▷▷ STARTING POINTS

- When Daddy and I went to the shops...
- Here is a mouse who...
- We're going on a crocodile hunt!
- One lonely caterpillar...
- Boom! went the thunder...

▷▷ CLUES FOR SUCCESS

- Look at some popular children's titles in a library or bookshop.
- Keep the plot simple.
- Familiar places like Grandma's house or playgroup are very important to toddlers. So are favourite toys. Use them as settings and characters for your story.
- Write about things which happen to little ones. At least one very successful book is about potty training!
- Use lists: letters, numbers, events or objects in your plot.
- Your story *must* have a happy ending.

▷▷ REDRAFTING AND IMPROVING

- Read your story aloud to another person, the younger the better.
- Read it again. Note all the points where they join in with you.
- Check the length – if the listener fidgets, it is too long.
- Check the plot – if the listener can retell the story to you, then you've got the level right.
- Add more repeat phrases if your reader finds it hard to join in. Soft gentle whispers and loud, shout-me-out words will also help.
- Check that you have used some onomatopoeia.
- Make adjustments and read aloud again, to a toddler if possible.
- When you are sure that your story is right, make it into a book. Have fun including pictures, flaps, cut-outs, or fold-outs or even pop-ups.

≫ WRITING FRAMES

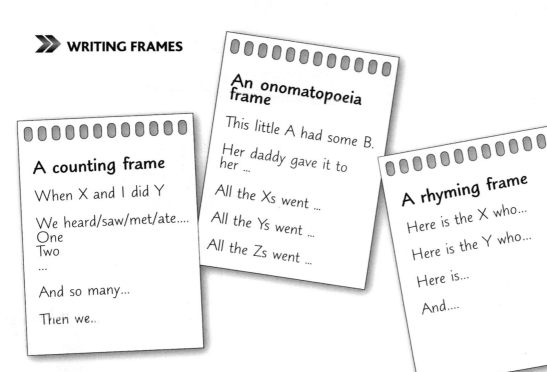

A counting frame

When X and I did Y

We heard/saw/met/ate.....
One
Two
...

And so many...

Then we..

An onomatopoeia frame

This little A had some B.

Her daddy gave it to her ...

All the Xs went ...

All the Ys went ...

All the Zs went ...

A rhyming frame

Here is the X who...

Here is the Y who...

Here is...

And....

Other frames could be: *letters of the alphabet, searching for a small friend, times of the day, rooms in the house,* etc.

6 ▷ Looking back

- **Onomatopoeia** is when words describe sounds. Children's writers use them a lot because they are fun to hear and say.

- **Plot** is what we call a storyline. Some books and plays have a main plot and sub-plots which branch off from the main story. However, books for toddlers will only ever have one very simple plot.

- **Rhyme, rhythm and repetition** add enjoyment to books for young children. They help them to join in with books meant for reading aloud.

Laughter and language

1 ▷ **Purpose**

In this unit you will:

- read an extract from a television comedy series
- learn about the features of scriptwriting
- write your own sketch based on a historical event

▷▷ **Subject links:** *drama, media studies, history*

2 ▷ **Television script**

Blackadder the third: Ink and Incapability

Scene Three – Prince George's Chambers

As the extract opens Blackadder has just announced the arrival of Dr Johnson.

BLACKADDER	I'm sorry, sir. I merely wished to congratulate Dr Johnson on not having left out a single word. *He smiles at Johnson, Johnson glares.* Shall I fetch the tea, my lord?
PRINCE GEORGE	Yes, yes – and get that damn fire up here, will you.
BLACKADDER	*Smoothly.* Certainly, sir. I shall return … interphrastically. *A smug nod and he leaves.*
PRINCE GEORGE	So, Dr Johnson. Sit ye down. Now, this book of yours. Tell me, what's it all about?
JOHNSON	It is a book about the English language, sir.
PRINCE GEORGE	I see. And the hero's name is what?
JOHNSON	There is no hero, sir.
PRINCE GEORGE	No hero? Well! Lucky I reminded you! Better put one in pronto. Call him George, that's a good name for a hero. What about heroines?
JOHNSON	There is no heroine, sir – unless it is our Mother Tongue.
PRINCE GEORGE	Ah – the mother's the heroine. Nice twist. So how far have we got then? Old Mother Tongue is in love with George the hero…Now what about murders? Mother Tongue doesn't get murdered, does she?

JOHNSON	No, she doesn't! No one gets murdered! Or married! Or in a tricky situation over a pound note!
PRINCE GEORGE	Well, now, look Dr Johnson, I may be as thick as a whale omelette, but even I know that a book's got to have a plot.
JOHNSON	Not this one, sir. It is a book that tells you what English words mean.
PRINCE GEORGE	But I know what English words mean. I speak English. You must be a bit of a thicko!
	That is it. Johnson is seriously angry. He rises to his feet.
JOHNSON	Perhaps you would rather not be patron of my book, sir, if you can see no value in it whatsoever!
PRINCE GEORGE	Perhaps so, sir, since it sounds to me as though being patron of this complete cowpat of a book will set the seal once and for all on my reputation as an utter turnip head.
JOHNSON	It is a reputation well deserved, sir! Farewell. *He marches towards the double doors and flings them open. Blackadder is revealed very calmly.*
BLACKADDER	Leaving already, Doctor? Not staying for your pendigestatory interludicule?
JOHNSON	No, sir, show me out!
BLACKADDER	Certainly, sir. Anything I can do to facilitate your velocitous extramuralization.
JOHNSON	*To Prince George.* You will regret this doubly, sir. Not only have you impeculiated *he glares with self-satisfaction at Blackadder, who is not impressed* my dictionary, you have also lost the chance to act as patron to the only book in the world that is even better.
BLACKADDER	And what's that, sir? *Dictionary 2: The Return of the Killer Dictionaries?*
JOHNSON	No, sir – it is *Edmund: A Butler's Tale* by Gertrude Perkins.

R Curtis, B Elton, R Atkinson and J Lloyd

3 Key features

The writers:

- use unusual vocabulary and a mixture of modern and old-fashioned phrases to create humour
- do not need to use speech punctuation
- set out the writing in a special way to show the differences between speech and action

- What sort of book does Prince George think that Johnson has written?
- Why is Johnson annoyed with George, and how does Blackadder anger him further?
- Writers sometimes use pen names (pseudonyms). Who do you think Gertrude Perkins really is?

51

4 > Language skills

Word

Writers create new words if they cannot find one that fits their need. Some newly-invented words, called **neologisms** or **coinages**, do become part of the language: *television* and *Internet* are both twentieth-century coinages.

Nonce words are new words which are invented and used only once. The words highlighted in yellow in the text are all nonce words. You will not find them in modern dictionaries, and they were not in Dr Johnson's first English Dictionary either.

❶ Look at how words appear in a dictionary. Usually you are given:

- the word, and sometimes a guide to pronouncing it,

- the **word class** – noun, adjective, verb etc. sometimes called **parts of speech**

- a definition or meaning

- the **etymology** – the history of the word or how it came to be formed from other words.

❷ Look up the following words in a dictionary and write out the definitions:

facilitate	*molecule*
impeach	*gustatory*
impecunious	*gestation*
ridicule	*peculiar*

❸ Write a dictionary definition to explain the meaning of each of the nonce words highlighted in yellow in the text.

Work out what the words mean from the way they are used in each sentence. They may look or sound like words you already know. Here is a definition of the first word as an example:

word: *interphrastically*
word class: *adverb*
meaning: *'within the space of a short conversation'*
etymology: *comes from* inter- *as in 'interval' and* phrasis *which is Greek for 'to speak'*

Spelling

The suffix *-tion* is used to make nouns from verbs:

gestate ➜ gestation
operate ➜ operation
locate ➜ location

The sound of *-tion* is always 'sh'n'.

❶ Find two *-tion* words from the text and say which verbs they have been created from.

Sentence

Television and **playscript punctuation** is not the same as dialogue punctuation in prose writing.

A **script** does not need speech marks. Instead the writer uses different **emphases** to show how each part of the script is used. Emphases can be **bold type**, *italics*, underlining, CAPITALS or other types of print.

In the extract, CAPITAL LETTERS are used for the names of the characters.

The words the actor must speak appear in normal print.

The stage directions appear in *italics*. They tell the actor where, when and how to move, or how to say the lines.

> *Johnson is seriously angry.*
> *He rises to his feet.*

JOHNSON Perhaps you would rather not be patron of my book, sir, if you can see no value in it whatsoever!

❶ Write out the following lines as script, using the right emphases.

Blackadder comes into the room to find Prince George standing in front of a raging fire. Blackadder very politely says to the Prince, 'Your Highness…may I offer my congratulations.'

The Prince replies, 'Thanks Blackadder!' and goes on with a contented laugh to call Dr Johnson a pompous baboon. The Prince does not think he will be back in a hurry.

Text

Verbal humour is humour which comes from what the characters say, rather than from comic situations. A character might say something and another character takes the wrong meaning.

JOHNSON There is no heroine, sir – unless it is our Mother Tongue.

PRINCE GEORGE Ah – the mother's the heroine. Nice twist.

The audience understands the correct meaning all along. This kind of misunderstanding makes the audience laugh at the second character.

❶ Write down other points about Dr Johnson's book which Prince George fails to understand. Whom do you laugh at most?

Humour can also come from the way that characters behave towards one another.

Dr Johnson knows that he is more clever than the Prince and is certain that his book is perfect. Prince George is rather silly and not very well-educated. Johnson gets angry at his stupidity. They both seem very foolish.

❷ What does Blackadder say to make Dr Johnson seem even more of a fool? Talk in pairs about why you find this funny.

5 ▷ Planning your own writing

1 Write a short playscript which is based on an incident in history.

2 Include at least one historical character; you may invent other characters.

3 Choose your historical moment carefully. Or use one from the list below.

4 Pinpoint a moment of humour: it could be a misunderstanding between two characters.

5 Think up a dramatic ending.

▷▷ CLUES FOR SUCCESS

● Read up on your chosen historical moment first and use the facts you discover.

● List the characters.

● Set the scene or location for the action.

● Concentrate on what the characters say to one another in the first draft.

● Keep stage directions limited – just exits and entrances.

● Word process your script. You can then print off several copies later.

▷▷ STARTING POINTS

● King Canute commands the waves to turn back. Two of his courtiers look on.

● King Alfred burns the cakes. The peasant woman who is sheltering him comes back to find a house full of smoke.

● Admiral Nelson is dying aboard his flagship. Second in command Hardy comforts him. Who else is there?

● Elizabeth I steps onto the cloak which Walter Raleigh has laid across a puddle. Her lady in waiting fusses.

● The Montgolfier brothers land at the end of their first balloon flight. A very angry farmer appears.

● Florence Nightingale arrives at the field hospital. Two overworked army doctors can't believe they've sent a woman.

▷▷ REDRAFTING AND IMPROVING

1 Try out your scene with friends. If you have word processed your writing, print a copy for each person.

2 Read the script aloud to hear whether the speeches sound natural. Get advice from your readers. What would be easier to say? (You don't have to make all the changes they suggest.)

3 Add in more stage directions. They tell the actors where and when to move: *sitting down, walks to the table.* They also give instructions about how the words are spoken: *softly, to the audience.*

4 Check that you have used the correct emphasis: CAPITALS for names, *italic* for stage directions.

>> WRITING FRAMES

- List the characters (names in capitals), then describe each one briefly.

- Set the scene or location.

- Enter character(s), or if they are already on stage begin the speeches.

- The first few speeches must tell your audience what the story is to be about.

- Use questions and answers between the characters to give information.

- Continue the conversation, leading up to the misunderstanding or problem that the characters face.

- Add a further character now. They may enter or be discovered, eavesdropping like Blackadder.

- The new character may help to clear up the misunderstanding or solve the problem – or they might make things worse!

- Finish your scene with all or some leaving the stage or set. Or close the curtain, or freeze the frame.

PRINCE GEORGE *heir to the throne of England*

Scene 3 - Prince George's Chambers.

Enter **DR JOHNSON**

Now this book of yours.

Tell me, what's it about?
It is a book about the English Language, sir.

...even I know that a book's got to have a plot.
Not this one, sir. It is a book that tells you what English words mean.

BLACKADDER *is revealed very calmly.*

And what's that, sir?
Dictionary 2...?

Exeunt omnes/Exit Curtain/Freeze.

---

6 > Looking back

- **Script punctuation** is not the same as speech punctuation in prose writing. A **script** does not need speech marks.

- **Emphases** are used to show: CHARACTERS' NAMES, the words which the actor will speak aloud *and how he or she should speak or move*.

- **Humour** can be created through comic situations, misunderstandings or the way characters behave towards one another.

Other people's lives

In this unit you will:

- learn about the special features of autobiographical writing
- discuss how detail can make people and situations seem real
- write a section from your own autobiography

▶▶ **Subject links:** *history, media studies, PSE, ICT*

2 ▶ **Autobiography**

'My grandmother's house' from *Letter to Daniel*

I spent most of my childhood summers living with her in St Declans....

I remember many things about that house: the smell of brown bread baking in the kitchen, collecting armfuls of apples in the garden for crab apple jelly, picking blackcurrants for jam, playing endless games of 'kiss or torture' with my friends' sisters, choking desperately on my first cigarette in the shed at the end of the garden while my grandmother laughed to herself in the kitchen.

On rainy afternoons my grandmother would bring down the big box of toy soldiers collected over the years by her own sons and I would lose myself in imaginary battles and conquests. Later, when I saw a girl I wanted to ask out, it was my grandmother who gave me the courage to venture forth, a teenage Romeo in brushed denim jeans, and suggest a trip to the cinema. 'The worst she can say is no,' she told me and, as always, she was right. In fact the girl said 'Yes', and our relationship lasted, believe it or not, for eight years. When we broke up and I was plunged into extended youthful misery my grandmother was waiting in St Declans with a mug of cocoa and a sympathetic smile.

I left Cork and the world of my childhood in 1979 and began a journalistic career that would take me to places my grandparents had barely heard of. As the years went on, I saw less and less of my grandmother. Yet each time I came back to St Declans she seemed to be the strong warm person I had always known. And then, while living in Belfast, I received news that she was suffering from cancer. When I went to see her she seemed frail and suddenly old, and she told me she believed she was dying. 'I'm on the way out Ferg,' she said and then added, 'but we all have to go some time.'

My grandmother was eventually transferred to the Royal Marsden Hospital in London where the doctors seemed more optimistic. At about the same time I was appointed BBC correspondent in South Africa, a job I had wanted from the moment I joined the Corporation. My grandmother was delighted for me and even spoke hopefully of being there to greet me at St Declans when I came home in the summer.

On our way out to South Africa my wife and I stopped off in London to visit her at the Royal Marsden. There, among other old people, in a city she did not know, my grandmother seemed small and vulnerable, a little old lady for whom unseen shadows were lengthening every day. We spoke about the past and about our large group of relatives, and she told me to take care of myself and my wife, Anne. 'Mind that little girl,' she joked.

When I got up to go I noticed that my grandmother had tears in her eyes and we both knew, without saying a word, that I would never see her again. She took my hand in hers and whispered into my ear, 'Always remember, love, that I will be watching out for you, wherever you are, always.'

A month later she came home to die. I was given the news early one morning on a long-distance call from Ireland. I walked out into the garden and cried for a long time. And then, with the birds of the highveld singing their hearts out, I went back inside and woke my wife. We sat for hours drinking tea and remembering my grandmother, and I am happy to say that most of the memories involved laughter.

Fergal Keane

3 ⟩ Key features

The writer:
- uses the first person – I – to tell his own story
- arranges the story chronologically so that events follow the normal passage of time
- gives detailed descriptions to help the reader imagine people and situations

≫
- Who is narrating the story?
- In which country does most of the story take place? Which other countries are talked about?
- Pick out two sentences which tell you something about the writer's personality.

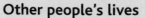

4 Language skills

Word

When we want to avoid using phrases which sound rude or uncomfortable we use **euphemisms**.

1 What do these phrases from the extract really mean?

> *I'm on the way out*
> *we all have to go sometime*
> *unseen shadows were lengthening*
> *passed on*

Explain why the writer uses these euphemisms rather than the more direct meanings you found.

2 Make a list of other euphemisms with similar meanings.

3 Collect as many euphemisms as you can for the following awkward ideas:

- feeling unwell: *under the weather, off colour...*

- being lazy or not turning up for work or school: *swinging the lead...*

Spelling

Suffix *-ally*: When an adjective ends with the letters *-ic*, you form the adverb from it using the suffix *-ally*.

> *sympathetic + -ally sympathetically*
> *journalistic + -ally journalistically*
> *optimistic + -ally optimistically*

In speech you do not pronounce the *-al* of *-ally*.

1 Make adverbs from the following adjectives, by adding -ally:

> *basic*
> *specific*
> *realistic*

2 The exception to the rule above is the adjective *public*. Check in a dictionary the correct spelling of the adverb formed from it. Learn the exception.

Sentence

The **first person** is the one who is writing or speaking, using the **personal pronouns** *I*, *we* or *us*.

In autobiographical writing, the writer tells us about his or her own life, writing in the first person.

The writer uses the first person singular – *I* – when writing just about himself:

> *As the years went on, I saw less and less of my grandmother.*

He uses the first person plural – *we* – when he is not alone in the story:

> *We sat for hours drinking tea and remembering my grandmother.*

❶ Write a short paragraph about something you did today with your friends, to practise using the first person.

If we add a word or phrase to a sentence, using commas, brackets or dashes, we say that the word or phrase is in **parenthesis**. (To pronounce it, put the stress on the *-ren-*.)

The writer of the extract uses pairs of commas to show where he has included extra detail.

> *Later,* when I saw a girl I wanted to ask out, *it was my grandmother who gave me the courage to venture forth,* a teenage Romeo in brushed denim jeans, *and suggest a trip to the cinema.*

❷ Find three further examples of commas marking out information in parenthesis in the extract.

Text

Verb tenses let you know the time when something happens: either in the past, the present or the future. Almost all of the extract is written in the past tense, because the events are already over.

❶ Rewrite the commentary below in the past tense, as if you were reporting for the sports page.

> *Jones passes the ball to Evans. Evans dribbles, hesitates, then shunts it along the wing. The direction of play is changing. Williams spots it, picks it up now, turns, shoots.. and she scores!*

A **chronological** narrative starts at the earliest event in the story and moves on through time.

Inexperienced writers, like young children, often link their sentences and paragraphs very simply like this:

> *Then... and then... and then...*

Later they learn how to keep the reader interested by using different phrases to begin their sentences and paragraphs. These phrases are known as **time adverbials**, because they show the passing of time.

❷ Find and list phrases from the extract which show time moving on. Begin with:

> *In 1970...*
> *As the years went on...*
> *At about the same time..*
> *On our way out to South Africa...*

5 ▷ Planning your own writing

Write a short section of your own autobiography, in which you talk about another person. Use one of the writing frames to start your draft. Choose the one which best suits your storyline and personality.

▷ STARTING POINTS

- moments you remember with a friend or relative still close to you

- memories of someone you rarely, or no longer, see

- recollections of a teacher, club-leader or other important adult in your life

- incidents which reveal why your best friend is so special

- disastrous times with a brother, sister or friend

▷ CLUES FOR SUCCESS

- Decide who will be reading your work.

- Match your writing to your intended reader (or listener).

- Select a few detailed memories.

- Write in the first person.

- Arrange your events in a chronological way.

- Include details of time and place.

April 2nd
This morning mum got a letter from her brother in S.Africa. We haven't heard from uncle Pete for eight months, so she was really pleased.

Met max at corner of New Road. Stopped at newsagents for cans of Cola. Saw Billy— Not speaking still.

April 4th
At the moment, I'm getting on really well with my maths. Mrs Evans, our new teacher, says I should be able to catch up what I've missed before the end of term. GOOD NEWS!

➤➤ WRITING FRAMES

Style a: Autobiographical Narrative   **Style b:** Diary or Journal

This piece will be chronological, with a story shape, written in paragraphs. It will use mostly statements. Personal pronouns, especially I, will appear often. Most of it will be in the past tense.

This piece will take a day-by-day structure, perhaps each day beginning with a date – *Monday 2nd*. Sentences can be in shorthand form and will probably be shorter. Personal pronouns can sometimes be left out altogether. Some of it will be in the present tense.

You can use these constructions or devise your own.

I remember...
In those days...
Each week...
Every Saturday..
At about the same time...

This morning...
Met Max at the corner of New Road
At the moment...
Tomorrow...
One of these days...

➤➤ REDRAFTING AND IMPROVING

- How does your personality come across? Have you involved your reader?

- Are the events set out in chronological order? Have you kept to the same tense?

- Have you used interesting adjectives or euphemisms?

- Are your sentences a good length, including some detail marked out by commas?

- Is your diary or journal layout easy to follow?

6 ▸ Looking back

- **Euphemisms** can be used to avoid being too blunt or rude about a topic. They may also add interest and colour.

- **The first person** is used whenever you write about yourself.

- More detail can be added to a sentence in **parenthesis**. Pairs of commas, dashes or brackets enclose the extra information.

Tuneful tales of times past

1 ▷ Purpose

In this unit you will:

- read three different types of ballad
- notice the common features and differences in ballads across the centuries
- write your own ballad – a story in verse

▶▶ **Subject links:** *music, art, history, drama*

2 ▷ Ballads

a traditional oral ballad – 'Black Jack Davy'

Late last night when the squire come home
Enquiring for his lady,
Some denied and some replied,
'She's gone with the Black Jack Davy.'

'So saddle to me the bonny brown steed:
The grey was never so speedy.
I would ride all day and ride all night
Till I catch that Black Jack Davy'

Oh he rode up hills and he rode down dales,
Over many a wild high mountain.
And they did say that saw him go,
'Black Jack Davy he is hunting.'

He rode east and he rode west,
All in the morning early,
Until he spied his lady fair
Cold and wet and weary.

'Why did you leave your house and land?
Why did you leave your baby?
Why did you leave your own wedded love
To go with the Black Jack Davy?'

Oh he rode up hills
    and he rode
    down dales,
Over many a wild
    high mountain.
And they did say
    that saw him go,
'Black Jack Davy
    he is hunting.'

'What care I for your goose-feather bed,
Your sheets and downs a-bravely,
When I may sleep on the cold hard ground
Along with the Black Jack Davy?

Then I'll kick off my high-heeled shoes
Made of Spanish leather
And I'll put on my lowland brogues
And skip it o'er the heather.'

Oh he rode up hills and he rode down dales,
Over many a wild high mountain.
And they did say that saw him go,
'Black Jack Davy he is hunting.' *Traditional*

b a lyrical ballad – 'Lord Ullin's daughter'

A chieftain to the highlands bound
Cries 'Boatman, do not tarry!
And I'll give thee a silver pound
To row us o'er the ferry!'

'Now who be ye would cross Lochgyle,
This dark and stormy water?'
'O, I'm the chief of Ulva's isle,
And this, Lord Ullin's daughter.

'And fast before her father's men
Three days we've fled together,
For should he find us in the glen,
My blood would stain the heather.

'His horsemen hard behind us ride –
Should they our steps discover,
Then who will cheer my bonny bride
When they have slain her lover?'

Out spoke the hardy Highland wight,
'I'll go, my chief, I'm ready:
It is not for your silver bright;
But for your winsome lady:

'And by my word! the bonny bird
In danger shall not tarry;
So though the waves are raging white
I'll row you o'er the ferry.'

By this the storm grew loud apace,
The water-wraith was shrieking;
And in the scowl of heaven each face
Grew dark as they were speaking.

But still as wilder blew the wind,
And as the night grew drearer,
Adown the glen rode armed men,
Their trampling sounded nearer.

Thomas Campbell 1777–1844

'O haste thee, haste!' the lady cries,
'Though tempests round us gather;
I'll meet the raging of the skies,
But not an angry father.'

The boat has left a stormy land,
A stormy sea before her, -
When, oh! too strong for human hand,
The tempest gathered o'er her.

And still they rowed amidst the roar
Of waters fast prevailing:
Lord Ullin reached that fatal shore,
His wrath was changed to wailing.

For sore dismayed through storm and shade,
His child he did discover: –
One lonely hand she stretched for aid,
And one was round her lover.

'Come back! Come back!' he cried in grief,
'Across this stormy water:
And I'll forgive your Highland chief,
My daughter! – O my daughter!'

'Twas vain: the loud waves lashed the shore,
Return or aid preventing:
The waters wild went o'er his child,
And he was left lamenting.

C a modern ballad – 'What has happened to Lulu?'

What has happened to Lulu, mother?
What has happened to Lu?
There's nothing in her bed but an old rag doll
And by its side a shoe.

Why is her window
    wide, mother,
The curtain flapping free,
And only a circle on the
    dusty shelf
Where her money-box
    used to be:

Why do you turn your
    head, mother,
And why do the tear-
    drops fall?
And why do you crumple
    that note on the fire
And say it is nothing at all?

I woke to voices late last night,
I heard an engine roar.
Why do you tell me the things I heard
Were a dream and nothing more?

I heard somebody cry, mother,
In anger or in pain,
But now I ask you why, mother,
You say it was a gust of rain.

Why do you wander about as though
You don't know what to do?
What has happened to Lulu mother?
What has happened to Lu?

Charles Causley 1970

3 ▸ Key features

The poets
- tell a story in verse
- use regular features such as rhyme, rhythm and repeated phrases
- include questions and conversations

>> ● Who is the rider in ballad **a**?
● Explain why Lord Ullin's daughter is afraid that father will catch up with her.
● How old do you think the child speaker is in ballad **c**? And how old is her sister, Lulu?

4 ▷ Language skills

Word

Words ending with the same (or similar) sounds are said to **rhyme**.

  feet/beat   *feather/whether*

These examples are called complete rhymes.

Words where the sounds are almost the same can be used as **half-rhymes**.

  carry/ferry   *lady/bravely*

Words which look as if they should rhyme, yet are pronounced differently, are called **eye-rhymes**.

  speak/break.

Rhymes are usually placed at the ends of lines of poetry. When rhymes appear in the middle rather than just at the end of a line of poetry we call them **internal rhymes**.

  Some denied *and some* replied

Assonance happens when words have the same vowel sounds, but not the same endings.

  like/bright
  home/phone
  catch that Black Jack

❶ List all the examples of half-rhyme in ballad **a**. Write down one example of complete rhyme from the same poem.

❷ Unlike ballad **a**, ballads **b** and **c** contain more complete rhymes than half-rhymes. In ballad **b** find two examples of half-rhyme. Which one is the eye-rhyme?

❸ Find two examples of internal rhyme from ballad **b**. Why do you think the writer uses these internal rhymes?

❹ Make some rhyme lists to help you with your own writing. Use these starter words and add to the lists:

  speed, steed, lead…
  bird, word, preferred…
  west, rest…
  skies, lies…

Spelling

The letter string *-igh* always represents the long vowel sound 'I' as in *light*.

❶ Find five *-igh* words in ballads **a** and **b**. You may not know the meaning of one of these words so check it in a dictionary.

Sentence

Direct speech is used when the writer sets out the exact words of a speaker. It appears inside speech punctuation marks.

  Parminder said, 'I thought you were going on holiday this week.'

Reported speech does not give us the exact words of a speaker. Instead a narrator tells us what someone else has said. There is no need for speech punctuation.

  Parminder told me she thought you were going on holiday this week.

Sentence

Ballads **a** and **b** both include direct speech conversations. Ballad **c** uses reported speech.

1 Reread ballad **c** and imagine the full conversation between the mother and her child.

2 Write out the narrator's questions from the poem as the child's words in direct speech, using speech punctuation:

> 'What has happened to Lulu, Mother?...'

3 Add the mother's answers, turning them from reported speech into direct speech:

> You say it is nothing at all
> will become
> 'It is nothing at all.'

4 Mother does not answer all of her child's questions. Add some extra answers and write out the whole conversation using direct speech.

Text

A ballad is a poem or song which tells a story. It usually includes some kind of dialogue, often with one character questioning another.

Ballad form is made up of stanzas (verses). Each stanza of a ballad usually contains four lines of regular rhythm.

The **rhyme scheme** is the pattern of rhymes in a poem. Regular rhyme schemes helped the poets who spoke their poetry, rather than wrote it down.

One such pattern is known as **alternate rhyme**:

> *And fast before her father's men*
> *Three days we've fled together,*
> *For should he find us in the glen,*
> *My blood would stain the heather.*

Here the first and third lines rhyme together, and the second and fourth. This pattern is also sometimes known as an *abab* scheme.

1 For each of the ballads, work out and describe the rhyme scheme.

Repetition happens when phrases or whole lines appear more than once in a poem.

2 Which of the three ballads do you think would be the easiest to learn by heart? What are your reasons for thinking that?

When a line or number of lines is often repeated in a poem it is called a **refrain**. It is rather like a chorus.

3 Write a four-line refrain for either ballad **b** or ballad **c**. At least two of the lines should come from the original poem.

5 ▷ Planning your own writing

Write your own ballad – a story in verse.

The ballads in this unit deal with love, loss and mystery. Other traditional subjects for ballads are:

- tragedies and natural or man-made disasters – *'The Gresford Disaster'*
- tournaments, battles or victories on land or at sea
- murders or kidnaps - *'Little Sir Hugh'*
- supernatural events – *'The Ballad of King Henry'*

Decide on the subject you want to tackle in your ballad and search for a good story. You could use a famous story, a fairy or folk tale or something from local history.

The broadsheet ballad writers of the 17th, 18th and 19th centuries found their stories in local news and gossip. Some of them were quite gruesome! Take a tip from them and scour your local newspapers for headlines and reports which would make good ballad material. Tabloid national newspapers are also another great source of ideas.

▷▷ STARTING POINTS

- Tragedy ideas: a rail disaster, plane crash, flood or earthquake
- Mystery ideas: ghostly sightings, strange disappearances of people or objects
- Victory or contest ideas: a world-class sporting match, a local tournament
- Love and loss ideas: an elopement, the untimely death of a well-loved person
- Murder and crime ideas: a kidnap, serial killings, a highway robbery or road rage
- Heroic ideas: the story of a local hero or heroine, how a sporting hero saved the day

▷▷ CLUES FOR SUCCESS

- Make a short, clear summary of your story in prose, or as a cartoon strip
- Divide your story into five sections:
  - an introduction
  - three main facts
  - a resolution (or how it turns out)
- Write one stanza for each section, following the writing frame
- Use only four lines in each stanza
- Rhyme only the second and fourth lines, using your rhyme lists to help you
- Do not worry about perfect rhymes

≫≫ WRITING FRAME

Stanza 1: introduction
Give the setting of the story; the time, the place or both.

> It was in the middle of the night...
> As I was walking along...
> You've heard of the Gresford
>   Disaster...

Or you could begin by introducing characters

> Lord Thomas he was a bold ...
> Lady Margaret was sitting in
>   her bower room
> The Skipper he stood beside
>   the helm

Stanzas 2 to 4: the action
Use questions and answers to set out each new piece of action or each new fact. The first two lines of each stanza should carry the question. The second two lines will carry the answer.

The questions will depend on the story you have chosen. Here is a stanza to use as a pattern:

> How came this blood on your shirt
>   sleeve?
> Oh dear son, tell me?'
> 'It is the blood of my old grey horse
> That ploughed the field for thee.'

This is the story of Edward who has accidentally killed his brother in a fight. He arrives home and his mother asks:

> 'How came this blood on your shirt
>   sleeve?
> Oh dear son, tell me?'

In the second half of the stanza Edward replies, but not truthfully:

> 'It is the blood of my old grey horse
> That ploughed the field for thee.'

In the next stanza (3) Edward's mother repeats her question, and he tells her a different lie. When she finally repeats the question (stanza 4), Edward at last tells his mother the truth.

In your fourth stanza you should include the most vital piece of information about the story.

Stanza 5: the resolution
The final stanza should explain how everything turns out. The last lines of the stanza could be spoken by one of the characters

> 'When the sun sets under the
>   sycamore tree
> And that shall never be.'
> 'Those are the banks of Hell,
>   my love,
> Where you and I must go.'

REDRAFTING AND IMPROVING

1 Read your ballad to a friend or teacher, asking for some comments on the story. What else would they like to know about it?

2 Make some notes on new ideas to include.

3 Add to your ballad in any of these ways:

- Some stanzas immediately after the first one could give more information about setting or character.

- Include extra question and answer stanzas to give more facts about the story.

- Alternate the question and answer stanzas with some which explain actions.

    He rode up hill and he rode
      down dale
    And o'er many a wild wide
      mountain...

- Include more than one stanza of resolution.

4 Next concentrate on your rhyme scheme, checking that each second and fourth lines of each stanza rhyme.

- Repeat a whole phrase
- Or try out some internal rhymes instead.

5 Look out for lines or whole stanzas which would make a good refrain.

6 Read your ballad aloud again before making final changes. This time concentrate on the rhythm of the stanzas. The flow of the words should feel regular. If you are not sure, try singing your ballad to the tune of a song you already know (such as *Scarborough Fair* or *The Streets of London*).

6 ▶ Looking back

- **Ballads** tell stories in verse.

- There are two types of ballad: **traditional oral ballads**, originally passed on by word of mouth, and ballads which were **deliberately composed** and written down by poets or songwriters.

- All types of ballad use **rhyme**, **rhythm** and **repetition**, in the form of repeated phrases or refrains, to help the speaker or singer remember them.

Happily ever after

1 ▶ **Purpose**

In this unit you will:
- read and compare the beginnings and ends of novels
- learn how to close a story effectively
- write your own story endings

▶▶ **Subject links:** *art, music, history, geography, RS*

2 ▶ **Novel starts and novel endings**

a Skellig

I found **him** in the garage on a Sunday afternoon. It was the day after we moved into Falconer Road. The **winter** was ending. Mum had said we'd be moving just in time for the spring. Nobody else was there. Just me. The others were inside the house with Doctor Death, worrying about the baby.

He was lying there in the darkness behind the tea chests, in the dust and dirt. It was as if **he'd** been there forever. **He** was filthy and pale and dried out and I thought **he** was dead. I couldn't have been more wrong. I'd soon begin to see the truth about **him**, that there'd never been another creature like **him** in the world.

* * * * * * * *

> Narrative problems 1 and 2 – will the baby die? What is its name?

> Winter
> death
> darkness
> dust
> dirt
> dried out
> dead

> Narrative problem 3 – Who, or what, is **he**?

Answer/resolution 1

She looked down at the baby.

'She's beautiful', she gasped. 'She's extraordinary!'

And she looked around and laughed with us all.

She was really shy again when she said, 'I brought a present. I hope you don't mind.'

She unrolled a picture of Skellig, with his wings rising from his back and a tender smile on his white face.

Mum caught her breath.

She stared at me and she stared at Mina. For a moment, I thought she was going to ask us something. Then she simply smiled at both of us.

'Just something I made up', said Mina. 'I thought the baby might like it on her wall.'

'It's really lovely, Mina', Mum said, and she took it gently from Mina's hands.

'Thank you', said Mina. She stood there awkwardly. 'I'll leave you alone now.'

I led her back to the door.

We smiled at each other.

'See you tomorrow, Mina.'

'See you tomorrow, Michael.'

I watched her walk away in the late light. From across the street, Whisper came to join her. When Mina stooped down to stroke the cat, I was sure I saw for a second the ghostly image of her wings.

Back in the kitchen, they were talking again about giving the baby a proper name.

'Persephone', I said.

'Not that mouthful again', said Dad.

We thought a little longer, and in the end we simply called her Joy.

David Almond

beautiful
laughed
smile
light
Persephone
Joy

Answer/resolution 2

Is this a new narrative problem?

Sequel or left unresolved.

Answer given/suggested earlier in story: an angel?

b The Village by the Sea

When Lila went out on the beach it was so early in the morning that there was no one else there. The sand was washed clean by last night's tide and no one had walked on it except the birds that fished along the coast – gulls, curlews and sandpipers. She walked down to the sea with the small basket she carried on the flat of her hand, filled with flowers she had plucked from the garden around their house – scarlet hibiscus blooms, sweet-smelling spider lilies and bright butter-yellow allamanda flowers.

When she came to the edge of the sea, she lifted the folds of her sari and tucked them up at her waist, then waded out into the waves that came rushing up over her feet and swirling about her ankles in creamy foam. She waded in till she came to a cluster of three rocks. One of them was daubed with red and white powder. It was the sacred rock, a kind of temple in the sea. At high tide it would be inundated but now, at low tide, it could be freshly consecrated. Lila took the flowers from her basket and scattered them about the rock, then folded her hands and bowed.

* * * * * * * *

After the races, when the crowds had thinned, Hari still stood on the dunes and saw a group of women coming down the path with small flat baskets on the palms of their hands. They were walking down the beach to the three rocks that stood in the sea. He watched them wade into the peacock blue and green sea, the foam breaking against their ankles, to scatter flower petals and coloured powder on the rocks as they prayed to the sea. He saw that his mother was amongst them.

'Lila, look!' he said. 'Look, Lila.'

Anita Desai

3 ▷ Key features

The writers:
- make links between the ending and the opening
- answer questions or resolve problems set up at the start
- look forward to the future as well as back to the past

- How are Hari and Lila related?
- What do you think Lila prays for at the beginning of the story?
- Why do you think Hari calls out excitedly?

4 > Language skills

Word

Linked vocabulary is used in stories to help the reader follow the events and ideas. Chains of the same word or same phrase can be traced through the text, linking the end of the story to its beginning. The words highlighted in yellow in the extracts from *Skellig* show how this works.

Sometimes the chain is made up of different words but they will all be mentioning the same thing or person:

> *John   he   his   him*

The chain can also be made up of words linked by a similar meaning or something in common:

> *flowers   blooms   petals*

1 Look at the linked vocabulary shown in yellow for *Skellig*. Then pick out the words and phrases which link the opening and the ending of *The Village by the Sea* and list them. Compare your choices with those of another student.

Connotation happens where words suggest more than their main meaning to us. The words *winter* and *spring* are the nouns or names for two of the seasons of the year. Yet they both have connotations. *Winter* also suggests other ideas to us, such as snow, ice, cold, bare earth, death and even old age!

2 List any other ideas that you associate with *winter*. Make a separate list for the connotations of *spring*.

3 Make some connotation posters for the words in 3 and *rose*, *autumn*, *yellow*, *night*. Put your word, or a picture, in the centre of the poster and surround it with all the associated words and phrases you find.

Spelling

The vowel pattern *-au-* can be found at the start or in the middle words. Here are some words using *-au-* to learn and find the meaning of:

daub	*launder*
haul	*audience*
exhaust	*augment.*

1 Find as many more *-au-* words as you can and add them to your spelling list.

Sentence

The **hyphen** is a punctuation mark which joins two words together to make one word or a complete expression.

chocolate-brown   *two-year-old*
fox-hunting   *re-cover*

Adding or leaving out a hyphen will change the meaning of the word or phrase.

1 Compare these two sentences:

> *The two-year-old cats were pretty.*
> *The two year-old cats were pretty.*

Explain how taking out one hyphen from the second sentence has changed the meaning.

2 What are the differences between these paired words and expressions?

> *fox hunting – fox-hunting*
> *resign – re-sign*
> *dark chocolate-brown –*
> *dark-chocolate brown?*

Write a sentence for each word to show the differences in meaning.

3 Find two hyphenated expressions in extract **b**. How would their meanings be different if they did not have the hyphens? Write sentences including each pair of words.

Dashes (–) show that something extra has been added to a sentence.

4 There are two examples of sentences which use a single dash followed by extra material in extract **b**. Find them and copy out the sentences in full.

5 Now underline the word in the first part of each sentence which is made clearer by the dashes, as in this sentence:

> *The beach was crowded with grounded <u>boats</u> – flat-bottomed skiffs, jaunty dinghies and even a lop-sided catamaran.*

Text

Closure is the way a writer ends the story. Closures usually contain links with the beginning of a story. Words and phrases used at the end which remind us of the start help the reader feel satisfied with the ending.

1 Read all the extracts again and discuss whether you think the book in extract a or extract b offers the best closure. Explain your opinions on this.

Narrative problems are set up by the author at the start of a story. They are questions which need answers or problems which the characters will need to solve. They form the basis of the plot.

Resolutions are the answers to narrative problems. The author needs to resolve the problems before the story can end. Usually, some of the problems are resolved as the story progresses, rather than all of the questions being answered at the end. However, a story will have a very strong ending if the author reminds us of all the resolutions as part of the closure.

2 Look at the text of *Skellig* and notice the three narrative problems in the opening, marked in orange. Follow the arrows to the resolutions in the ending.

3 At the end of *Skellig* the author seems to set up another problem:

When Mina stooped down to stroke the cat, I was sure I saw for a second the ghostly image of her wings.

Note down whether you are happy to leave the question posed by this problem unanswered. Does it weaken or strengthen the ending? Explain your view in a short paragraph.

Coda is originally a musical term. It means a passage which rounds off the whole piece neatly. In writing the coda repeats some of the details of the opening paragraphs.

4 Make a chart to show the coda used to close the book in extract **b**. Begin like this:

Opening detail	Closing detail	Exact repeat	Changes
small basket	small flat baskets	no, but close	plural & shape of basket

Sequels are stories, books or even films which continue from where an earlier story left off. If a writer intends to produce a sequel to a story, she or he will give some hints, usually at the end, to suggest that there will be more to follow.

5 Reread the endings of the two books. Which one suggests that there will be a sequel? Write a brief outline of what you think might happen if the story continued in a follow-up book.

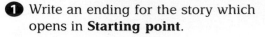

5 > Planning your own writing

1 Write an ending for the story which opens in **Starting point**.

2 Read the opening closely.

Study the sentences which give the story outline.

3 Write the ending from the moment that Buddy and his mum return home from the Court hearing of the trial.

4 Use material from the opening paragraphs in your ending.

5 Resolve the narrative problems or answer the questions.

6 Make your ending a happy one.

>> **STARTING POINT**

Buddy stole the money from his mother's purse just before he left for school. His mother was in the kitchen clearing up the breakfast things and
5   his father was still in bed.

He tiptoed into the front room and slipped the purse out of her handbag. He clicked it open and took out a £5 note. A wave of disgust swept through
10   him. Only two weeks ago he'd vowed to himself that he was going to stop shop-lifting and here he was stealing from his own mother. He hadn't done that since he was a little kid and had
15   sometimes nicked the odd ten pence. He was turning into a real thief. There must be something the matter with him. First, the shop-lifting. He'd done it a couple of times with some other
20   boys from school. They had stopped but he'd gone on doing it alone. And now, this.

He heard his mum come out of the kitchen and, in a moment of panic,
25   he fumbled with the catch on the purse. It wouldn't close properly so he just chucked it back in the bag still open. He put the handbag back on the sofa, crumpled the note into
30   his pocket, and went out of the room. His mum was in the hall putting on her coat.

Nigel Hinton

What happens in the rest of the story?...

- Buddy is thirteen. He is named after the singer Buddy Holly, as his dad is a big fan.

- Dad spent some time in prison in the past.

- Finding out the theft, his mum says, 'Like father, like son,' and leaves home.

- Buddy's dad does his best to look after him – he works 'nights'.

- Buddy tries to help save his dad from a life as a burglar.

- His plans go wrong and dad is arrested.

- Buddy runs away for a while, and eventually finds his mum.

- They return home, to find that dad is on trial for burglary.

If you have read the story before, and would like to try a different ending – go ahead.

CLUES FOR SUCCESS

- Find the narrative problems in the opening before you plan your ending. Your ending must answer any questions they raise.

- Note any details in the opening that you could repeat to form a coda. Details of character or setting are very good for this.

- Keep the ending simple. Close the story: do not ask new questions.

- Add extra detail – using dashes.

WRITING FRAMES

When Buddy got home…	Describe what Buddy does and says to his mum who has been to the trial.
His mum shrugged and…	How does she react?
'They let me see him for a bit afterwards. He asked me…'	What news will she give Buddy? Continue their conversation.
Buddy tried to imagine…	Buddy thinks about the future.
Mum managed a real smile. 'He said we had to…'	What instructions did Buddy's dad leave for them?
Buddy made the tea and they…	How does the story end? Think about the things people do to get back to normal after life has gone wrong.

REDRAFTING AND IMPROVING

Compare your version of the ending with that of another student. What did you both include? Where did you differ from one another? Answers to these questions will help you see where to change, add or cut material in your ending.

Write a second (alternative) ending to the story.

1 Begin at the same point, but this time leave something unresolved or a question unanswered.

2 It does not have to be a sad ending, but it will mean that not everything will work out perfectly.

3 Point the action forward, as if there will be a sequel. Which problem or question will you carry into the future? Or is there a new question? A new problem?

You might like to know that there is a sequel to *Buddy*, called *Buddy's Song*.

6 ▷ Looking back

- **Closure**, linking the end to the beginning of a story, is very important to the reader. Words and phrases used at the end of the story which mirror the start help the reader feel satisfied with the ending. The writer needs to plan both the opening and the ending very carefully to make good links.

- **Narrative problems** are questions which need answers or problems which the characters in a story will need to solve. They form the basis of the plot.

- **Resolutions** are the answers to those narrative problems. The author needs to resolve the problems before the story can have a satisfactory end.

- **Coda** is a passage which rounds off a whole piece neatly. It repeats some of the details of the opening paragraphs.

- **Sequels** continue from where an earlier story left off.

Glossary

Allusion The use of a word or phrase to refer to another story or idea.

Assonance The repetition of vowel sounds.

Ballad A poem or song which tells a story. Usually includes some kind of dialogue, with one character questioning another.

Ballad form Made up of stanzas (verses). Each stanza of a ballad usually contains four lines of regular rhythm with a rhyme scheme.

Closure The way a writer ends the story. Closures usually contain links with the beginning of the story.

Coda A passage which rounds off a piece neatly. The coda repeats some of the details of the opening paragraphs.

Colloquial English Informal, everyday speech and writing.

Connotation The connection in meaning that a word or phrase has with another word or phrase.

Euphemisms A mild or pleasant-sounding way of avoiding a rude or uncomfortable phrase.

First person When you are writing something from your own viewpoint, using the pronouns *I* or *we*, you are writing in the **first person** of the verb.

Genre A particular kind of writing with its own special features.

Homophones Words which sound the same or similar, but which have different spellings and meanings.

Imperative sentences Sentences that tell you or ask you to do something.

Onomatopoeia The name given to a word that sounds like its meaning.

Reported speech Words that are spoken by a character, but which are reported by the narrator, rather than reproduced word-for-word.

Rhyme scheme The pattern of rhymes in a poem.

Sequels Stories, books or films which continue from where an earlier story left off.

Time adverbials Adverbial phrases which show the passage of time.